THE NEW WEISS METHOD FOR BASSOON
VOLUME II

Douglas E. Spaniol
based on the work of Julius Weissenborn (1837-1888)

including new editions of
Weissenborn's *Studies for Advanced Students*, Op. 8, No. 2
Milde's *Studies on Scales and Chords*, Op. 24
Bona's *Complete Method for Rhythmical Articulation, Part II*

and selected exercises from
Weissenborn's *Studies for Beginners*, Op. 8, No. 1
Arban's *Complete Method*

Cover Image: Bassoon Engraving from Weissenborn's *Praktische Fagott-Schule* (1887)

ISBN: 978-1-5400-3592-9

Contact Us:
Hal Leonard
7777 West Bluemound Road
Milwaukee, WI 53213
Email: info@halleonard.com

In Europe contact:
Hal Leonard Europe Limited
42 Wigmore Street
Marylebone, London, W1U 2RN
Email: info@halleonardeurope.com

In Australia contact:
Hal Leonard Australia Pty. Ltd.
4 Lentara Court
Cheltenham, Victoria, 3192 Australia
Email: info@halleonard.com.au

To my three main bassoon teachers and mentors:
E. Sanford Berry, William Waterhouse, and Christopher Weait.

4

Table of Contents

Preface

For well over a century, students have learned to play the bassoon using Christian Julius Weissenborn's (1837–1888) instructional materials, arguably the most successful and most important pedagogical compositions ever written for bassoon. Despite their success, most editions of these materials have strayed significantly from Weissenborn's original pedagogical plan.

Perhaps most common among Weissenborn's teaching material is his *Praktische Fagott-Schule (Practical Bassoon-School* or *Practical Method for Bassoon)*. Its widespread use and longevity have earned it nicknames such as "The Bassoonist's Bible" and are a testament to the quality and sound pedagogy of Weissenborn's work.
The New Weissenborn Method for Bassoon (Hal Leonard, 2010; revised 2013) sought to provide bassoon students and teachers with better instructional material by returning to Weissenborn's original intent and content of the *Method*, as well as updating it and (in a few cases) expanding it for today's bassoonist. The pedagogical success of *The New Weissenborn Method (NWM)* has led to the creation of this second volume, *The New Weissenborn Method – Volume II (NWM II)*. Its aims are similar to the original volume: to look to the original intent and content of Weissenborn's work and to update and expand it as needed, in order to provide high quality instructional material for bassoonists – in this case for advanced bassoon students who have completed the first volume.

Christian Julius Weissenborn[1] (known as Julius) was born in Thuringia in 1837 to a musical family. His father, Johann Weissenborn (1788–1865) was a bassoonist in Thuringia. His much older brother, Friedrich Louis (1813–1862), played bassoon in the Leipzig orchestra from 1835–1855, and viola from 1855–1860. Although not the principal bassoonist, Friedrich appeared as soloist with the orchestra on eight occasions, receiving excellent reviews.[2] Like his father and brother, Julius Weissenborn was a successful bassoonist, achieving success at a young age. It is believed that he was playing professionally in Rostock in 1854 (age ca. 17), followed by work in St. Gallen, Eisenberg, and Düsseldorf. In 1856, at the tender age of 20, Weissenborn began in the prestigious position of principal bassoonist in the Leipzig Gewandhaus Orchestra, with whom he appeared as soloist in 1869, 1876, and 1879. In 1882 he was appointed as the first bassoon teacher at the Royal Conservatory of Music in Leipzig. He retired from the orchestra in 1887, and passed away in 1888 at the age of 51.

In addition to his work as bassoonist and teacher, Weissenborn was highly regarded as a well-rounded musician, especially as a composer and arranger. His compositions include works for piano, wind band, orchestra, and vocal ensembles. Perhaps his most profound work is *Die Drei*, a cantata for vocal soloists, choir, and orchestra, which was premiered in Leipzig in 1874. He also composed a set of six bassoon trios and many works for bassoon and piano.

---

[1] The majority of biographical information about Julius Weissenborn currently available in English is found in works written by William Waterhouse. These include the "Weissenborn" entry in *The New Grove Dictionary of Music and Musicians*, the preface to the *Studies for Advanced Students*, Op. 8, No. 2 (Universal Edition), the liner notes for *Romanze of Weissenborn* (Equilibrium EQL 72), and "New Light on the Weissenborn Family" *(The Double Reed*, Vol. 30, No. 2). Except where noted, information in this biographical sketch is derived from these sources.
[2] Hodges, Woodrow Joe. *A Biographical Dictionary of Bassoonists Born Before 1825*, 2 vols. Ph.D. Dissertation, University of Iowa, 1980.

Weissenborn's pedagogical materials for bassoon include *Studies for Beginners*, Op. 8, No.1; *Studies for Advanced Students*, Op. 8, No. 2; and the *Practical Method*. He also composed a set of at least eleven works for bassoon and piano, which he intended as a set of *'Tone- and Performance-Studies.'* Based upon evidence from some of Weissenborn's surviving manuscripts, William Waterhouse surmised that the *Method*, the two sets of etudes in Op. 8, and the *Tone- and Performance-Studies* were conceived as a grand three-part instructional curriculum for bassoonists. One could also conclude that the original three-part curriculum consisted of the *Studies for Beginners*, *Studies for Advanced Students*, and the *Tone- and Performance-Studies*, and that the *Method* later replaced the *Studies for Beginners* as the first part of the curriculum. Assuming this is the case, Weissenborn intended students to complete the *Method*, and then move on to the *Studies for Advanced Students*. Hence, *NWM II* uses the *Studies for Advanced Students* as the foundation for its content and organization.

NWM II contains all of Weissenborn's Op. 8, No. 2 studies, introduces keys and new notes in the same order, and (like Op. 8, No. 2) is divided into two main sections: "Studies in All Major and Minor Keys" and "Virtuosity Studies." *NWM II* also expands these studies with materials in corresponding keys, including long tones, scales, and arpeggios (much of which is based the Op. 8, No. 1 studies), and rhythmic etudes by Pasquale Bona. The last two lessons include exercises on multiple tonguing by Jean-Baptiste Arban. Each lesson also refers students to etudes from Ludwig Milde's *Studies on Scales and Chords*, Op. 24 (again, in corresponding keys), which are provided in the back of the book as a supplement akin to the Supplement of scale and chord studies in Weissenborn's *Practical Method*. These Milde studies are presented in a new edition that corrects wrong notes and clarifies accidentals. It also expands the set to include all fifteen key signatures (as does Op. 8, No. 2), as well as chromatic etudes in various keys. Lastly, most of the individual lessons direct students to important orchestral excerpts for bassoon, coordinated to match the keys and/or range of that lesson.

The following system of octave designation is used in this book:

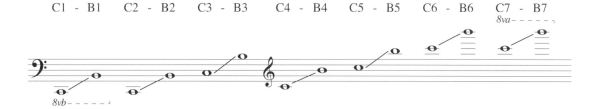

It is hoped that *NWM II* will become the centerpiece of a successful curriculum for advanced bassoon students and their teachers. A student who works with a skilled teacher and practices the material in this book diligently should develop control of the full working range of the bassoon; mastery of the basic vocabulary of tonal music (major and minor scales and common arpeggios); the ability to play in any key; and the ability to meet the technical, rhythmic, and artistic demands of music through the end of the Romantic era. Because today's professional bassoonists are expected to have additional skills, especially those required to meet the demands of 20th- and 21st-century 'classical' music and music of other genres, it is hoped that teachers and students will supplement this book with additional materials to develop these skills.

Doug Spaniol
Indianapolis, Indiana, 2019

Source Materials and Editing Procedures

Weissenborn – *Studies for Advanced Students*, Op. 8, No. 2

The sources for the material from Weissenborn's *Studies for Advanced Students*, Op. 8, No. 2 as found in *NWM II* are Weissenborn's original thematic catalog (described below) and the first edition published by C.F. Peters in or around 1887.[3]

It was mentioned in the Preface that most editions of Weissenborn's teaching materials strayed significantly from his original pedagogical plan. Perhaps in no case is this more true – and more detrimental – than in the case of the *Studies for Advanced Students*. These etudes have become known as the *50 Advanced Studies* and have become a staple of bassoon instruction, auditions, and competitions. Peters' original edition has been reprinted many times by several different publishers. Although this is testament to the pedagogical and musical quality of Weissenborn's etudes, that well-known and oft-used edition is substantially different from what Weissenborn originally intended.

In 1987, Universal Edition (Vienna) published an edition of these etudes by William Waterhouse entitled *Bassoon Studies, Op. 8/2 for Advanced Students (Original Version)*[4]. In the preface to this edition, Waterhouse explains that some of Weissenborn's surviving manuscripts came to light in 1982. Included in these manuscripts was a thematic catalog with an incipit and a brief description of each etude. A review of this thematic catalog quickly reveals numerous differences between Weissenborn's original design and the *50 Advanced Studies* as published by Peters and others:

- Most importantly, Op. 8, No. 2 originally consisted of 60 (not 50) studies. Ten studies were omitted from the Peters edition and are now lost.[5]

- Weissenborn's division of the set into two parts – 53 studies in all major and minor keys followed by seven 'Virtuosity Studies' – was done away with.

- Weissenborn's logical ordering of etudes by key (pairing relative major and minor and progressing from zero to seven accidentals in the key signature) was also undone. As a result, etudes appeared in a nearly random order.

- Six etudes appeared in different keys from those in the original.

- Several of the etudes had different tempo markings and/or initial dynamic markings.

A solid argument can be made that Weissenborn's original design is far superior. It is impossible to ascertain why the Peters edition varied from Weissenborn's original intention. Whatever the reason, it's sad to think that a century's worth of bassoon students have been deprived of Weissenborn's original design.

NWM II is built around the sound pedagogical principles of Weissenborn's original design: studying music in a logical ordering by keys, followed by more virtuosic music with increasing challenges in speed, technique, and range. Most lessons in *NWM II* contain one set of related keys (i.e. C Major and A Minor). Within the lessons, the 50 surviving etudes are presented in the order they were intended as shown by the thematic catalog. *However* – bassoonists may need to perform etudes as they appeared in the Peters 1887 edition, most likely for a competition or audition. For this reason,

---

[3] Weissenborn, Julius. *Fagott-Studien: op. 8. 2, Für Vorgeschrittene (Bassoon Studies for Advanced Pupils, Op. 8, No. 2)*. Leipzig: C.F. Peters, undated. (The plate number is 7123. Based upon this information it is surmised that this was published in 1887.)

[4] Waterhouse, William. *Bassoon Studies, Op. 8/2 for Advanced Pupils*. Vienna: Universal Edition, 1987.

[5] For reconstructions of these ten lost etudes, see: Weissenborn, Julius, edited by Doug Spaniol. *Bassoon Studies for Advanced Students, Opus 8,2*. Warngau: Accolade Musikverlag, 2012.

etudes that were transposed appear in both keys: the original keys according to the thematic catalog, and the keys in which they appeared in Peters 1887. The transposed etudes appear in *NWM II* in the lesson that covers the key to which they were transposed; students or teachers may opt to skip these etudes. If an etude has different tempo markings in the two sources, both markings are clearly marked. Because ten original etudes have been lost, there are three keys (G♯ Minor, F♯ Major, A♯ Minor) for which there is no Weissenborn advanced study available; in these instances, an etude from Weissenborn's Op. 8, No. 1 has been substituted.

Despite the obvious flaws in the Peters 1887 edition related to the order of the etudes, their keys, and their tempo markings, it remains the only source for the actual etudes themselves. Hence, *NWM II* adheres to the musical notations in Peters 1887 when it comes to notes, rhythms, dynamics, articulations, etc. **For reference, the chart on p. 14 provides complete information on the etudes as they appear in the thematic catalog, in Peters 1887 ("50 Advanced Studies"), and in *NWM II.*** It should clarify the above information and help users locate etudes as needed.

Weissenborn – *Studies for Beginners,* Op. 8, No. 1

The source of the material from Weissenborn's *Studies for Beginners*, Op. 8, No. 1 as found in *NWM II* is the original edition published by Peters in or around 1887.[6]

Section III of the *Studies for Beginners* is entitled "The scales in the 24 keys most commonly used." For each key there is a short study in long tones, one or two short scale exercises, and then an etude in that key. This general plan was somewhat co-opted for *NWM II*, where each lesson begins with long tones, scale and arpeggio exercises, and then etudes in both the major key and relative minor key. Most of the long tone studies and some of the scale exercises in *NWM II* are derived from Op. 8, No. 1. However, they are expanded to fit the increased range, and other modifications were made as necessary.

As mentioned above, there are three keys for which there is no surviving etude from Op. 8, No.2. In these instances, an etude from Op. 8, No. 1 was substituted with transpositions made as necessary.

Bona – *Complete Method for Rhythmical Articulation, Part II*

The sources for the material from Bona's *Complete Method for Rhythmical Articulation, Part II* as found in *NWM II* are the fourth edition of Bona's *Metodo Completo per la Divisione*,[7] and the English translation of the fourth edition published by White-Smith Music Publishing in 1905, titled *Complete Method for Rhythmical Articulation.*[8]

Pasquale Bona (1808–1878)[9] wrote *Metodo Completo per la Divisione* as a training book for all music students, not for bassoonists specifically. The term *'divisione'* had been used historically to refer to embellishments or ornaments. In the White-Smith edition, it has been translated into English as *'rhythmical articulation.'* One should note that Bona's book is intended for training in sight-singing, solfeggio, and rhythm – not for articulations as bassoonists typically use the term (i.e. staccato, legato, etc.). It is included in *NWM II* for additional practice in sight-reading and rhythm. The

[6] Weissenborn, Julius. *Fagott-Studien: op. 8. 1, Für Anfänger (Bassoon Studies for Beginners, Op. 8, No. 1).* Leipzig: C.F. Peters, undated. (The plate number is 7122. Based upon this information it is surmised that this was published in 1887.)

[7] Bona, Pasquale. *Metodo Completo per la Divisione.* Milan: F. Lucca, undated. (Plate number 26506.)

[8] Bona, Pasquale, English Translation by Ambrose Davenport. *Complete Method for Rhythmical Articulation, Fourth Italian Edition.* Boston: White-Smith Publishing Co., 1905.

[9] Pasquale Bona." https://en.wikipedia.org/wiki/Pasquale_Bona. n.d., Accessed July 27, 2018. This article cites this reference: Andrea Sessa, Il melodramma italiano 1861-1900. Dizionario bio-bibliografico dei compositori, Olschki, Firenze 2003, p. 56.

most appropriate etudes for this aim are found in Part II; hence, those are the etudes contained in *NWM II*.

Bona's etudes have here been liberally edited. In the aforementioned sources, the etudes have very few dynamic and articulation markings; these have been added to make the etudes more musical and idiomatic and to present additional sight-reading challenges. In addition, the etudes have been changed from treble to bass clef and transposed to match the key of the lesson in *NWM II*.[10] Finally, the range of the etudes has been expanded to match the range of the bassoon and the range of the lessons, especially to include any recently introduced high notes.

Arban – *Complete Method*

The source of the material from Arban's *Method* is *Complete Method for the Cornet*, published by J.W. Pepper in 1879 and revised by T. H. Rollinson.[11] The preface to that edition states that "Mr. Rollinson…has erased some of the Surplus Exercises… and has endeavored to give the Student just the matter that Arban has written to make a thorough Musician." In other words, the Rollinson revision is an abridged edition of Arban's original *Method*.

Jean-Baptiste Arban (1825–1889) was a French cornetist, conductor and teacher.[12] His *Method* is to cornetists and trumpeters what Weissenborn's *Method* is to bassoonists: the most widely-used instructional text for over a century. Its exercises on double- and triple-tonguing are particularly effective for initial practice of these techniques. For *NWM II* these exercises have been transcribed for bassoon and transposed to appropriate keys when necessary. The number of exercises in Rollinson's abridged version is more than sufficient for initial practice; a few more have been omitted from *NWM II*. Students are also referred to other etudes and excerpts for additional practice. It should be noted that Arban introduces triple-tonguing first, followed by double-tonguing; *NWM II* reverses this order.

Milde – *Studies on Scales and Chords*, Op. 24

It was mentioned in the Preface that Weissenborn's instructional materials are "arguably the most successful and most important pedagogical compositions ever written for bassoon." If one were to have such an argument, the other contender would be Ludwig Milde. Because these studies are such an integral part of advanced bassoon study, and because they match the level of difficulty, range, and organization of *NWM II* well, it has been decided to include them here.

It was not possible to ascertain when and where these etudes were first published. (Milde's *Concert Studies*, Op. 26 were published by Merseburger of Leipzig in or around 1895;[13] it is surmised that the *Studies on Scales and Chords* were published around the same time and place.) There is a well-known edition that has been reprinted several times and that is familiar to virtually all bassoonists; presumably these are reprints of the original edition.[14] The primary source for the materials from Milde's *Studies on Scales and Chords*, Op. 24 as found in *NWM II* is that edition.

---

[10] It should be noted that I came to know of these etudes from an edition for bass clef instruments edited by William D. Fitch and published by Carl Fischer in 1969. I have used the Fitch edition in my teaching for many years. In creating this new edition, I consciously avoided referring to the Fitch edition so as not to duplicate his articulation and dynamic markings.

[11] Arban, Jean-Baptiste, revised by T.H. Rollinson. *Method for the Cornet*. Philadelphia: J.W. Pepper, 1879.

[12] Tarr, E. (2001, January 01). Arban, (Joseph) Jean-Baptiste. Grove Music Online. Ed. Retrieved July 27, 2018 from http:////www.oxfordmusiconline.com/grovemusic/view/10.1093/gmo/9781561592630.001.0001/omo-9781561592630-e-0000001162.

[13] McGill, David. "Milde has a FACE!" (*The Double Reed*, Vol. 30, No. 3, pp. 71-75). Baltimore, MD: International Double Reed Society, 2007.

[14] This includes editions by Kalmus, Cundy-Bettoney, and others. See bibliography for full details.

Other editions consulted include an anonymously edited and undated edition by Hofmeister of Leipzig,[15] an edition by Simon Kovar published by International Music Company of New York,[16] and a recent edition edited by Benjamin Kamins and William Short published by Theodor Presser.[17]

Bassoonists know well that most older editions of these etudes are littered with errors and ambiguities, especially regarding accidentals and the octaves to which they apply. One of the primary aims of this edition is to remedy that situation. In this edition, accidentals apply only to the octave in which they appear. For the sake of clarity, courtesy accidentals are often provided to cancel accidentals from a different octave. Courtesy accidentals are not provided after clef changes. Accidentals appearing in brackets indicate that it is unclear which note Milde intended; the accidental in brackets is the editor's suggestion. In some cases, notes have been respelled enharmonically to conform to rules of music notation; this is especially true in chromatic scale passages. Slurs added by the editor are dashed; grace notes added are in brackets.

What makes this edition unique, however, is not the detailed editing work described above, but rather that it has nine additional etudes for a total of 34 instead of the original 25. Six of these etudes were added to include the keys of Gb Major, C♯ Major, and Cb Major. (Milde did not include etudes in these key signatures in his set, despite the title of "Studies in all Keys" that appears in many editions.) Each of these six etudes is a transposition of another etude in the set, i.e. the etudes in G Major were transposed down a half step to create etudes in Gb Major. One of the beneficial qualities of Weissenborn's *Studies for Advanced Students* (and hence *NWM II)* is that it covers all 30 major and minor keys. With these additions, the Milde scale and chord studies now do as well. Milde's chromatic scale etude (#25) was also transposed to appear not only in C Major but also in Bb Major, B Major, and Db Major. This was done to help assure mastery of chromatic scales no matter the starting point, nor which notes fall on strong beats or strong parts of the beat.

To illustrate the information in the preceding paragraphs, and to help users locate etudes, the chart found on p. 16 provides complete information on these Milde etudes as they appear in *NWM II*.

Orchestral Excerpts

Orchestral excerpts are an important component of advanced bassoon study. I believe students are better served by studying orchestral excerpts using complete scores and bassoon parts whenever possible. Hence, no orchestral excerpts are included in *NWM II*; rather, students are referred to appropriate excerpts (based upon key, range, and topic) at the end of lessons. Despite the fact that orchestral excerpts do not actually appear in *NWM II*, I would like to acknowledge Brett van Gansbeke's website, The Orchestral Bassoon (www.orchestralbassoon.com) as an important source of information and encourage all bassoon students to use this outstanding resource in their study of orchestral repertoire.

---

[15] Milde, Ludwig. *Studien über Tonleiter- und Akkord-Zerlegungen für Fagott, op. 24.* Leipzig: VEB Friedrich Hofmeister, undated. (plate # 7381)

[16] Milde, Ludwig, ed. by Simon Kovar. *25 Studies in Scales and Chords, Opus 24.* New York: International Music Company, 1950. This appears to be a reprint of the original edition with dynamics and a few other markings added by Kovar.

[17] Milde, Ludwig, ed. by Benjamin Kamins and William Short. *25 Studies in Scales and Chords, Op. 24.* King of Prussia, PA: Theodor Presser Company, 2017. It is highly recommended that students consult the Kamins/Short edition for helpful information on how to best approach the study of these etudes and for numerous suggestions on fingerings and other techniques.

How to Use This Book

The *NWM* and *NWM II* are designed to bring Weissenborn's original curriculum to today's bassoon students, updated and expanded as needed.

NWM II is broadly designed to match Weissenborn's *Studies for Advanced Students*, Op 8, No. 2; that is, it begins with lessons organized by key in the same order and follows this with 'Virtuosity Studies.' The first 15 lessons generally mirror the format of the lessons in the *Studies for Beginners*, Op. 8, No. 1: long tones, followed by scale studies, then etude(s), all in the same key(s). The 'Virtuosity Studies' near the end of the book will help students master specific topics and techniques not covered earlier: chromatic scales, high notes, and multiple tonguing.

Each lesson is *NWM II* is quite long. Students should not be expected to prepare an entire lesson in one week nor cover an entire lesson in one session with a teacher. For Lessons 1–15 it may be useful to approach the work thusly: 1) major key material, 2) minor key material, 3) Bona, Milde, and excerpts.

Long Tones

In the *Studies for Beginners*, Weissenborn provided long tone exercises in a variety of formats, i.e. the range, lengths of notes, and dynamic schemes vary from key to key. *NWM II* adopts Weissenborn's format for each key, expanding the range as necessary. For keys that weren't covered in the *Studies for Beginners*, a more "generic" approach to long tone studies is presented.

Long tones form an important part of any serious woodwind player's practice and instruction. Teachers and performers often have their own method for practicing long tones. One should feel free to augment (or even substitute) the long tone studies here with studies of their own design.

However long tones are practiced, the goals should be clear – to develop good control, tone, and intonation of every note. Strive for clean note beginnings; steady, beautiful tone; controlled note endings; and good intonation throughout. Make sure to use proper fingerings, especially regarding proper use of the whisper key, half-hole, speaker keys, and resonance key. For notes where more than one fingering is used regularly, you should practice long tones with each fingering. Use of a tuner and/or drone is strongly recommended to aid intonation. One should strive to maintain the level of tone, control, and intonation developed in the long tone studies as they move on to the scale and arpeggio exercises and etudes.

Scales and Arpeggios

Similar to the long tone exercises, the scale exercises in Weissenborn's *Studies for Beginners* vary from key to key. The scale exercises in *NWM II* are similar but are presented in a consistent format, and are expanded to match the greater range being practiced. *NWM II* also includes major scales in thirds, minor scales in all three forms (natural, harmonic, melodic), and common arpeggios (tonic triad, tonic seventh chord, dominant seventh chord, and leading-tone seventh chord). Together, this covers the basic vocabulary for each key. By the end of Lesson 15, all major and minor keys have been covered. A student who works diligently through these exercises should develop fluency of the basic vocabulary of tonal music: all major and minor scales and triads, and all of the common types of seventh chords (major, dominant, minor, half-diminished, and fully-diminished).

Use of a metronome is highly recommended. Speed should be the last goal. First one should strive for rhythmic precision, healthy hand position, and efficient finger motions. Strive for consistency and ease. It is suggested that each exercise be practiced first slurred, then legato, then staccato. This order is designed to first establish good tone production and finger use, then finger/tongue coordination, and finally a good staccato – something that all bassoonists need!

It is recommended that, at first, students practice these exercises looking at the notes. It's important to develop the ability to recognize scales and arpeggios by sight when reading music. Once that is well-developed, students should work on playing these scales and arpeggios from memory.

Etudes

The etudes provide students an opportunity to employ the tone production developed in the long tones and the technique developed in the scales and arpeggios in a musical setting. The ultimate goal is to develop fundamentals of tone production and technique to the point where, in performance, one can focus on musical and artistic concerns instead of technical issues. Achieving this requires diligent, consistent, and effective practice, aided by quality instruction. The Weissenborn *Studies for Advanced Students* provide a wide variety of musical challenges and are excellent preparation for almost any musical challenge. A student who can perform each of these etudes well, both technically and musically, will be very well prepared indeed!

The etudes by Pasquale Bona are included primarily to add extra emphasis in rhythmic challenges and to develop sight-reading. Remember that you can only sight-read a piece of music once. Take advantage of that opportunity with all music, especially these etudes by Bona. Before sight-reading the piece, establish a strong internal sense of the tempo and meter. Conducting and counting out loud is an excellent way to achieve this. Also be sure to note the key and be 'thinking in that key' while playing. Lastly, scan the etude for any rhythms, dynamics, clef changes, etc. that may need special attention. Then sight-read the music top to bottom without stopping as if you were in a rehearsal or performance situation. Make note of any errors that need to be addressed and return to practice those spots. Strive to be able to play each etude accurately while keeping the tempo steady – both with and without a metronome.

At the end of each lesson in *NWM II*, students are referred to the corresponding Milde studies in the Supplement. These provide further opportunity to develop technical mastery of the instrument.[18] **Users of this book who wish to find specific Weissenborn or Milde etudes in *NWM II* can use the reference charts on pp. 14–16 to locate them easily.**

Orchestral Excerpts

Orchestral excerpts form an important part of serious bassoon students' study, in part because they form the basis of many auditions. In studying excerpts, students are encouraged to learn the *entire work*, rather than just the bassoon part or the few measures of the excerpt. The best ways to do this are to listen to recordings while reading the full score and to attend live performances when possible. Obtaining complete bassoon parts is far preferable then working from excerpt books. The Orchestral Bassoon (www.orchestralbassoon.com) mentioned earlier is an immensely valuable resource for the study of orchestral excerpts.

For reference, the chart on p. 17 lists the orchestral excerpts recommended in each *NWM II* lesson and relevant details.

---

[18]Again, it is recommended that students read the information in the Kamins/Short publication for suggestions on how to maximize the benefit of studying these (and all) etudes. .

Reference Charts

The charts on the following pages are provided to assist students and teachers in cross-referencing the primary and supplementary materials in *NWM II*.

I. **Weissenborn *Studies for Advanced Students,* Op. 8, No. 2** Lists each etude according to its organization/location in Weissenborn's Thematic Catalog, Peters' original edition, and *NWM II*.

II. **Milde *Studies on Scales and Chords,* Op. 24** Lists each etude by its original number, key[s], and *NWM II* lesson.

III. **Recommended Orchestral Excerpts** Lists all recommended excerpts along with the *NWM II* lesson in which each is referenced.

I. Weissenborn *Studies for Advanced Students,* Op. 8, No. 2						
Studies in All Major and Minor Keys						
Thematic Catalog		Peters 1887 ("50 Advanced Studies")			NWM II	
Etude Number	Key	Etude Number	Key (if different)	Notes	Lesson	Page
(54)		20	B♭ Maj	Originally #54 in C Maj	Review	20
1	C Maj	3			1	27
2	C Maj	1			1	27
3	C Maj	12			1	28
(22)		6	C Maj	Originally #22 in D Maj	1	29
4	A Min	13			1	30
5	A Min	26			1	30
6	F Maj	2			2	33
7	F Maj	7			2	33
(18)		14	F Maj	Originally #18 in G Maj	2	34
8	F Maj	21		Two tempo markings	2	35
9	D Min	22			2	36
10	D Min	15			2	36
11	B♭ Maj	16			3	40
12	B♭ Maj	8			3	41
13 (LOST)	(B♭ Maj)	n/a			n/a	n/a
14	G Min	10			3	42
15	G Min	17			3	42
(37)		23	G Min	Originally #37 in F♯ Min	3	43
16	G Maj	4			4	46
17	G Maj	18			4	47
18	G Maj	14	F Maj		4	48
19	E Min	37			4	49
20	E Min	19			4	50
21	D Maj	27			5	54
22	D Maj	6	C Maj		5	55
23	D Maj	32		Two tempo markings	5	56
24	B Min	5			5	57

Studies in all Major and Minor Keys *cont.*						
Thematic Catalog		**Peters 1887 ("50 Advanced Studies")**			**NWM II**	
Etude Number	*Key*	*Etude Number*	*Key (if different)*	*Notes*	*Lesson*	*Page*
25	B Min	33			5	58
26	E♭ Maj	9			6	62
27	E♭ Maj	24			6	63
28	C Min	30			6	64
29 (LOST)	(C Min)	n/a			n/a	n/a
30	A♭ Maj	34	A Maj	Two tempo markings	7	68
31	A♭ Maj	25			7	69
32	F Min	31		Two tempo markings	7	70
33 (LOST)	(F Min)	n/a			n/a	n/a
34 (LOST)	(A Maj)	n/a			n/a	n/a
35 (LOST)	(A Maj)	n/a			n/a	n/a
(30)		34	A Maj	Two tempo markings; originally #30 in A♭ Maj	8	74
36	F♯ Min	35			8	75
37	F♯ Min	23	G Min		8	76
38	E Maj	38			9	79
39	E Maj	36			9	80
40	C♯ Min	39			9	81
41 (LOST)	(C♯ Min)	n/a			n/a	n/a
42 (LOST)	(D♭ Maj)	n/a			n/a	n/a
(52)		40	D♭ Maj	Originally #52 in C♯ Maj	10	85
43	B♭ Min	41			10	86
44	B Maj	42			11	90
45 (LOST)	(G♯ Min)	n/a			n/a	n/a
from Op. 8, No. 1	G♯ Min	n/a			11	91
46	G♭ Maj	44			12	94
47	E♭ Min	45			12	96
48 (LOST)	(F♯ Maj)	n/a			n/a	n/a
from Op. 8, No. 1	F♯ Maj			Originally in G♭ *and* F♯ Maj	13	99
49	D♯ Min	43		Based on Beethoven #4	13	100
50	C♭ Maj	46			14	103
51	A♭ Min	47			14	104
52	C♯ Maj	40	D♭ Maj		15	107
from Op. 8, No. 1	A♯ Min	n/a		Originally in G Min	15	107
53 (LOST)	(A♯ Min)				n/a	n/a
Virtuosity Studies						
54	C Maj	20	B♭ Maj	Chromatic scale study	16	112
55	G Maj	28			17	114
56	G Maj	11		Based on Schumann #1	17	114
57	D Min	48		Introduces D5	18	120
58	E♭ Maj	49		Introduces E♭5	19	125
59	E♭ Maj	29			19	126
60	C Maj	50		Introduces E5	20	132

II. Milde *Studies on Scales and Chords,* Op. 24

Etude Number	Key	Scale/Chord Study	Notes	Lesson in NWM II	Page
1	C Major	Scale	Also transposed to C♯ for #24C	1	142
2	C Major	Chord	Also transposed to C♯ for #24D	1	143
3	G Major	Scale	Also transposed to G♭ for #24A	4	144
4	G Major	Chord	Also transposed to G♭ for #24B	4	145
5	F Major	Scale		2	146
6	F Major	Chord		2	147
7	D Major	Scale		5	148
8	D Major	Chord		5	149
9	B♭ Major	Scale	Also transposed to C♭ for #24E	3	150
10	B♭ Major	Chord	Also transposed to C♭ for #24F	3	151
11	A Major	Scale		8	152
12	A Major	Chord		8	153
13	E♭ Major	Scale		6	154
14	E♭ Major	Chord		6	155
15	E Major	Scale		9	156
16	E Major	Chord		9	157
17	A♭ Major	Scale		7	158
18	A♭ Major	Chord		7	159
19	B Major	Scale		11	160
20	B Major	Chord		11	161
21	D♭ Major	Scale		10	162
22	D♭ Major	Chord		10	163
23	F♯ Major	Scale		13	164
24	F♯ Major	Chord		13	165
24A	G♭ Major	Scale	Transposition of #3	12	166
24B	G♭ Major	Chord	Transposition of #4	12	167
24C	C♯ Major	Scale	Transposition of #1	15	168
24D	C♯ Major	Chord	Transposition of #2	15	169
24E	C♭ Major	Scale	Transposition of #9	14	170
24F	C♭ Major	Chord	Transposition of #10	14	171
25	C Major	Chromatic Scale		16	172
25A	B♭ Major	Chromatic Scale	Transposition of #25	Review (and 16)	174
25B	B Major	Chromatic Scale	Transposition of #25	16	176
25C	D♭ Major	Chromatic Scale	Transposition of #25	16	178

III. Recommended Orchestral Excerpts				
Lesson in NWM II	Key/Topic	Composer	Title	Movement/Section	Bsn Part
2	F Maj/D Min	Brahms	Violin Concerto	2 (opening)	2
		Tchaikovsky	Symphony No. 4	1 (mm. 294-300)	1
3	B♭ Maj/G Min	Beethoven	Violin Concerto	3 (mm. 134-158)	1
		Berlioz	*Symphonie Fantastique*	4 (mm. 49-63)	all
4	G Maj/E Min	Beethoven	Violin Concerto	2 (mm. 20-30)	1
		Tchaikovsky	Symphony No. 5	1 (solos after Q)	1
		Tchaikovsky	Symphony No. 6	1 (mm. 1-12)	1
5	D Maj/B Min	Prokofiev	*Peter and the Wolf*	solos	1
		Rimsky-Korsakov	*Scheherazade*	2 (mm. 5-26)	1
6	E♭ Maj/C Min	Beethoven	Symphony No. 5	3 (mm. 268-325)	1
		Shostakovich	Symphony No. 9	5 (mm. 1-27)	1
7	A♭ Maj/F Min	Dukas	*The Sorcerer's Apprentice*	Reh. 7–9	all
		Tchaikovsky	Symphony No. 4	1 (mm. 104-114)	1
8	C♯5/D♭5	Ravel	*Boléro*	Reh. 2–3	1
	A Maj/F♯ Min	Tchaikovsky	Symphony No. 5	3 (Reh. A–E)	1
9	E Maj/C♯ Min	Wagner	*Tannhäuser*	Overture (mm. 1-16)	1&2
10	D♭ Maj/B♭ Min	Donizetti	*L'Elisir d'Amore*	"Una furtiva lagrima"	1
		Dukas	*The Sorcerer's Apprentice*	Reh. 43-45	all
		Tchaikovsky	Symphony No. 4	2 (m. 274-end)	1
12	G♭ Maj/E♭ Min	Stravinsky	*The Firebird*	Berceuse	1
13	F♯ Maj/D♯ Min	Beethoven	Symphony No. 4	2	1
14	C♭ Maj/A♭ Min	Stravinsky	*The Rite of Spring*	Reh. 12	1
17	Miscellaneous Virtuosity Studies	Bartok	*Concerto for Orchestra*	2 (duet and trio)	all
		Ravel	Piano Concerto	3 (Reh. 14–16)	1&2
		Ravel	*Rapsodie Espagnole*	1 (Reh. 8–9)	1&2
		Rimsky-Korsakov	*Scheherazade*	2 (cadenzas)	1
		Schumann	Symphony No. 1	1 (solo after Reh. B)	1
		Strauss	*Till Eulenspiegel's Merry Pranks*	(see p. 117)	1
18	D5	Shostakovich	Symphony No. 9	4	1
		Stravinsky	*The Rite of Spring*	mm. 1-15	1
20	E5	Ravel	Piano Concerto	1 (Reh. 9–10)	1
21	Double Tongue	Beethoven	Symphony No. 4	4	1
		Berlioz	*Symphonie Fantastique*	5 (mm. 47-64)	all
		Mozart	*The Marriage of Figaro*	Overture	1
		Mendelssohn	*A Midsummer Night's Dream*	Scherzo (mm. 1-26)	1
		Smetana	*The Bartered Bride*	Overture	1
22	Triple Tongue	Mendelssohn	Symphony No. 4	1&4	1&2
		Ravel	*Bolero*	Reh. 4-5	1&2

Acknowledgments

I am greatly indebted to the late William Waterhouse for spurring my interest in Julius Weissenborn and aiding my endeavors to restore and update his pedagogical bassoon works. I am also forever indebted to his widow Elisabeth Waterhouse, who has been incredibly helpful and supportive in these efforts and in providing me continued access to the Weissenborn manuscripts.

In addition to William Waterhouse, I would like to express my gratitude to Christopher Weait and the late E. Sanford Berry. Their collective influence as my primary bassoon teachers and mentors can be seen throughout this book and in many other ways.

I would like to acknowledge again Brett Van Gansbeke and his excellent work on The Orchestral Bassoon (www.orchestralbassoon.com), which was very helpful in preparing this publication and is a great aid to bassoonists and their teachers everywhere.

I am grateful to all at Hal Leonard for their support and assistance, and especially to Laura Kohrs for her expertise, insightful ideas, and enthusiasm.

Lastly, I would like to thank the libraries of Butler University and Interlochen Center for the Arts whose collections, resources, and staffs greatly aided this publication.

Bibliography

Arban, Jean-Baptiste, rev. by T.H. Rollinson. *Method for the Cornet*. Philadelphia, PA: J.W. Pepper, 1879.

Bona, Pasquale. *Metodo Completo per la Divisione*. Milan: F. Lucca, undated. (Plate number 26506.)

Bona, Pasquale, English Translation by Ambrose Davenport. *Complete Method for Rhythmical Articulation, Fourth Italian Edition*. Boston: White-Smith Publishing Co., 1905.

Bona, Pasquale, ed. by William Fitch. *Rhythmical Articulation: Parts II and III from the Complete Method*. New York: Carl Fischer, 1969.

Cooper, Lewis Hugh and Howard Toplansky. *Essentials of Bassoon Technique (German System)*. Union, NJ: H. Toplansky, 1968.

Hodges, Woodrow Joe. "A Biographical Dictionary of Bassoonists Born before 1825." Ph.D. dissertation, University of Iowa, 1980.

McGill, David. "Milde has a FACE!" in *The Double Reed*, Vol. 30, No. 3, pp. 71-75. Baltimore, MD: International Double Reed Society, 2007.

Milde, Ludwig. *25 Studies in All Keys, Opus 24*. New York: Edwin F. Kalmus, undated. (no plate number)

_____. *25 Studies in All Keys, Opus 24*. Boston: The Cundy-Bettoney Co, undated. (Plate number 5474-26, handwritten.) This edition also appears in the Cundy-Bettoney edition of the Weissenborn *Method for Bassoon*.

_____. *Studien über Tonleiter- und Akkord-Zerlegungen für Fagott, op. 24*. Leipzig: VEB Friedrich Hofmeister, undated. (Plate number 7381.)

Milde, Ludwig, ed. by Simon Kovar. *25 Studies in Scales and Chords, Opus 24.* New York: International Music Company, 1950. (This appears to be a reprint of the original edition with dynamics and a few other markings added by Kovar.)

Milde, Ludwig, ed. by Benjamin Kamins and William Short. *25 Studies in Scales and Chords, Op. 24.* King of Prussia, PA: Theodor Presser Company, 2017.

"Pasquale Bona." https://en.wikipedia.org/wiki/Pasquale_Bona, n.d., accessed July 27, 2018.

Spaniol, Douglas E. and Julius Weissenborn. *The New Weissenborn Method for Bassoon: Based on Praktische Fagott-Schule (Practical Bassoon Method) by Julius Weissenborn.* Milwaukee, WI: Hal Leonard, 2010, revised 2013.

Tarr, E. (2001, January 01). Arban, (Joseph) Jean-Baptiste. Grove Music Online. Ed. Retrieved 27 Jul. 2018, from http:////www.oxfordmusiconline.com/grovemusic/view/10.1093/gmo/9781561592630.001.0001/omo-9781561592630-e-0000001162.

Van Gansbeke, Brett. *The Orchestral Bassoon.* Retrieved from http://www.orchestralbassoon.com.

Waterhouse, William. Preface to *Bassoon Studies, Op.8, Vol.2 for Advanced Pupils.* Vienna: Universal Editions, 1987.

_____. "New Light on the Weissenborn Family," *The Double Reed*, Vol.30, No.2, 2007, pp. 35–44.

_____. Liner notes to *Romanze of Weissenborn.* Equilibrium EQ 72, 2004.

_____. "Musicians and Graphic Artists: The Weissenborns of Leipzig and London." *Matrix: A Review for Printers & Bibliophiles*, no. 26, pp. 159-64. Risbury, Herefordshire: Whittington Press, 2006.

Weissenborn, Julius. *Practical Bassoon-School with Complete Theoretical Explanations for Teacher and Pupil.* Leipzig: R. Forberg, 1887.

_____. *Fagott-Studien: op. 8. 1, Für Anfänger (Bassoon Studies for Beginners, Op. 8, No. 1).* Leipzig: C.F. Peters, undated. (The plate number is 7122. Based upon this information, it is surmised that this was published in 1887.)

_____. *Fagott-Studien: op. 8. 2, Für Vorgeschrittene (Bassoon Studies for Advanced Pupils, Op. 8, No. 2).* Leipzig: C.F. Peters, undated. (The plate number is 7123. Based upon this information, it is surmised that this was published in 1887.)

Weissenborn, Julius, ed. by Fred Bettoney. *Method for Bassoon.* Boston: The Cundy-Bettoney Co., 1950. (Contains reprint of the Milde *Studies in All Keys, Opus 24.*)

Weissenborn, Julius, ed. by William Waterhouse. *Fagott-Studien: Op. 8/2. Für Fortgeschrittene.* Wien: Universal, 1987.

Weissenborn, Julius, ed. by Doug Spaniol. *Bassoon Studies for Advanced Students, Opus 8,2.* Warngau: Accolade Musikverlag, 2012.

West, Andrew. *From Solo Etude to Collaborative Duo: Creating Accompaniments to the 50 Concert Studies, Op. 26 for Bassoon by Ludwig Milde.* DMA Thesis, Texas Tech University, 2014.

Review
The New Weissenborn Method for Bassoon; B♭1 – B♭4

1. Long tones. Breathe/rest as needed.

Play each repeated passage three times: 1st time slurred, 2nd time legato, 3rd time staccato.

2. Chromatic Scale in Triplets on B♭

3. Chromatic Scale in Sixteenths on B♭

4. Thematic catalogue #54 (in C Major)/*50 Advanced Studies* #20 (in B♭ Major)

Allegro vivace (or any appropriate tempo for practice – D.E.S.)   C.J.W. Op. 8, No. 2

5. Sight-reading and Rhythm Study*: Bona *Method,* No. 75

Metodo Completo per la Divisione, Part II

*See author's suggestions for sight-reading on p. 13.

6. Play Etude No. 25A, Milde *25 Studies in Scales and Chords* (p. 174).

STUDIES IN ALL
MAJOR AND MINOR KEYS

Lesson 1
B4, C5, C Major and A Minor

New Notes

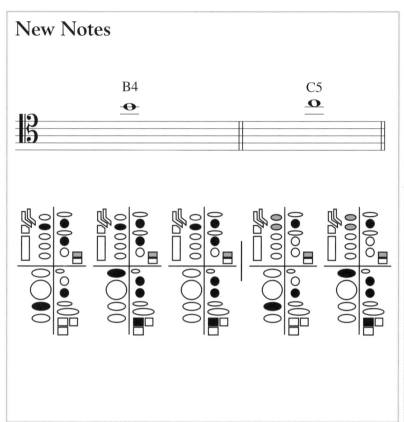

There are many ways to finger B4 and C5. Some of the most common options are shown here. Finding fingerings that speak well and are in tune can be problematic. Fingerings can vary greatly based upon the bassoonist, reed, and instrument.

For B4, the first fingering shown tends to be well in tune, but may be difficult technically depending upon the notes directly before or after. The second fingering tends to be sharp; the third fingering tends to be flat.

For both fingerings shown here, C5 may be vented with either the High C key, the High D key, or both. Experiment to find which combination works best. For bassoons without a High D key, using the High C key is the only option but should be sufficient. The first fingering shown tends to be in tune, but may be difficult technically depending upon the notes directly before or after. The second fingering tends to be sharp.

Note how similar the fingerings for B4 and C5 can be. For standard use, it's best to settle on fingerings that "match," like the first fingering for B4 and the first fingering for C5. Also note that the resonance key (Low E♭ key) is optional on all fingerings shown.

1. Introducing B4

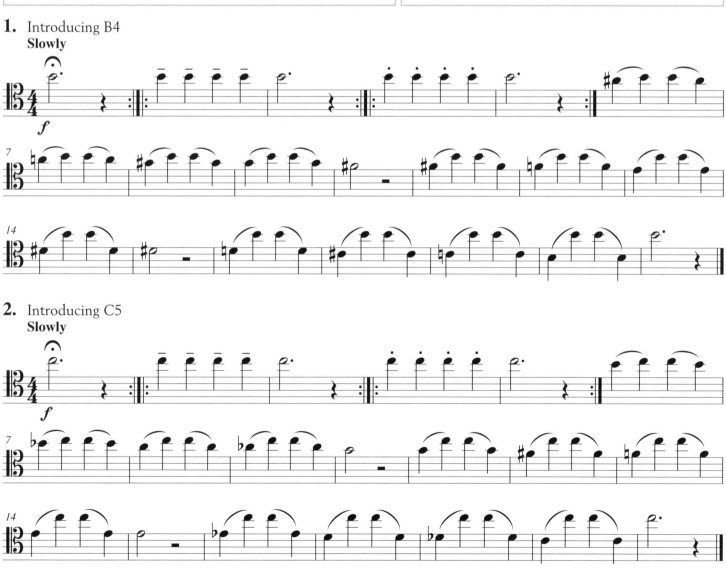

2. Introducing C5

3. C Major Long Tones. Breathe as needed.

Slowly

C.J.W. Op. 8, No. 1/D.E.S.

Play each repeated passage three times: 1st time slurred, 2nd time legato, 3rd time staccato.

4. C Major Scale

C.J.W. Op. 8, No. 1/D.E.S.

5. C Major Scale in Thirds

6. Tonic Major Triad (I, C)

7. Tonic Major Seventh Chord (I^7, C^{maj7})

8. Dominant Seventh Chord (V^7, G^7)

9. Leading-tone Half-diminished Seventh Chord (vii^{ø7}, b^{ø7})

10. A Minor Long Tones. Breathe as needed.

Sostenuto

C.J.W. Op. 8, No. 1/D.E.S.

Play each repeated passage three times: 1st time slurred, 2nd time legato, 3rd time staccato.

11. A Natural Minor Scale

C.J.W. Op. 8, No. 1/D.E.S.

12. A Harmonic Minor Scale

C.J.W. Op. 8, No. 1/D.E.S.

13. A Melodic Minor Scale

C.J.W. Op. 8, No. 1/D.E.S.

14. Tonic Minor Triad (i, A^m)

15. Tonic Minor Seventh Chord (i^7, A^m7)

16. Dominant Seventh Chord (V^7, E^7)

17. Leading-tone Fully-diminished Seventh Chord (vii°^7, g♯°^7)

18. Thematic catalogue #1/*50 Advanced Studies* #3

Allegro moderato

C.J.W. Op. 8, No. 2

19. Thematic catalogue #2/*50 Advanced Studies* #1

Allegro moderato

C.J.W. Op. 8, No. 2

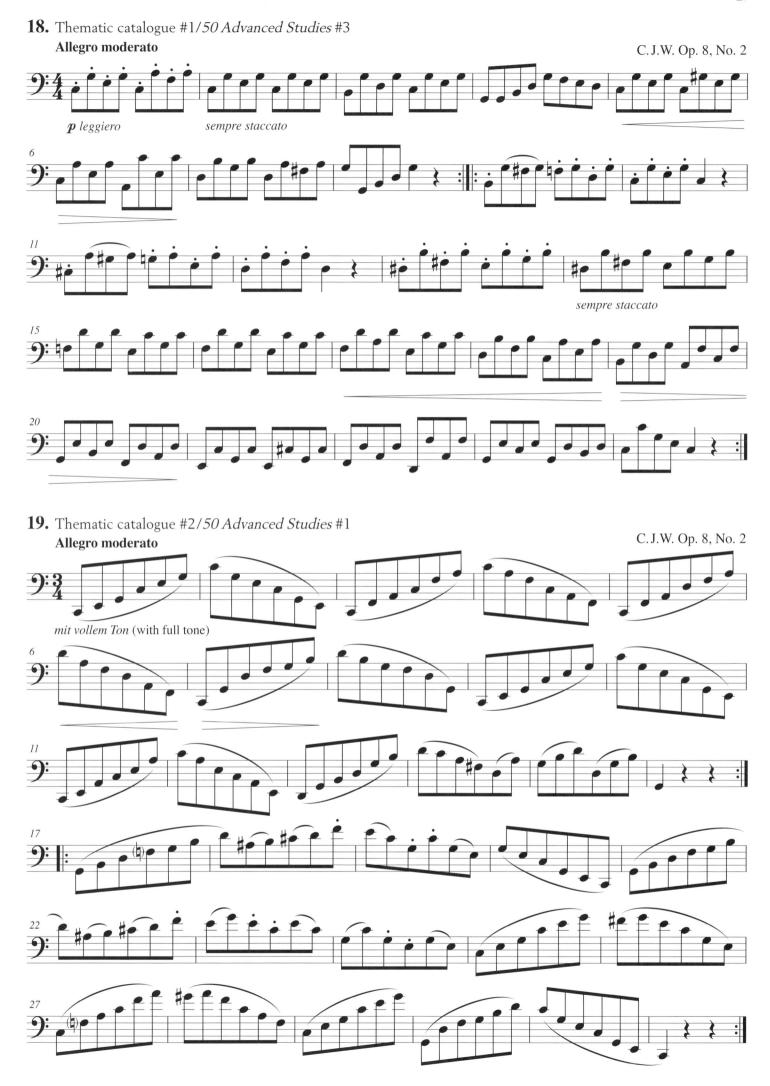

20. Thematic catalogue #3/*50 Advanced Studies* #12

Allegro

C.J.W. Op. 8, No. 2

21. Thematic catalogue #22 (in D Major)/*50 Advanced Studies* #6 (in C)

Allegretto grazioso

C.J.W. Op. 8, No. 2

22. Thematic catalogue #4/*50 Advanced Studies* #13

C.J.W. Op. 8, No. 2

23. Thematic catalogue #5/*50 Advanced Studies* #26

Scherzo
Allegro assai

C.J.W. Op. 8, No. 2

24. Sight-reading and Rhythm Study: Bona *Method,* No. 76

Metodo Completo per la Divisione, Part II

25. Play Etude No. 1, Milde *Studies in Scales and Chords* (p. 142).

26. Play Etude No. 2, Milde *Studies in Scales and Chords* (p. 143).

Lesson 2
F Major and D Minor

1. F Major Long Tones. Breathe as needed. — C.J.W. Op. 8, No. 1/D.E.S.

Play each repeated passage three times: 1st time slurred, 2nd time legato, 3rd time staccato.

2. F Major Scale — C.J.W. Op. 8, No. 1/D.E.S.

3. F Major Scale in Thirds

4. Tonic Major Triad (I, F)

5. Tonic Major Seventh Chord (I⁷, Fmaj7)

6. Dominant Seventh Chord (V⁷, C⁷)

7. Leading-tone Half-diminished Seventh Chord (viiø⁷, eø⁷)

8. D Minor Long Tones. Breathe as needed. — C.J.W. Op. 8, No. 1/D.E.S.

9. D Natural Minor Scale — C.J.W. Op. 8, No. 1/D.E.S.

10. D Harmonic Minor Scale — C.J.W. Op. 8, No. 1/D.E.S.

11. D Melodic Minor Scale

C.J.W. Op. 8, No. 1/D.E.S.

12. Tonic Minor Triad (i, Dm)

13. Tonic Minor Seventh Chord (i⁷, Dm⁷)

14. Dominant Seventh Chord (V⁷, A⁷)

15. Leading-tone Fully-diminished Seventh Chord (vii°⁷, c♯°⁷)

16. Thematic catalogue #6/*50 Advanced Studies* #2

C.J.W. Op. 8, No. 2

Allegretto (Tempo di Minuetto)

17. Thematic catalogue #7/*50 Advanced Studies* #7

C.J.W. Op. 8, No. 2

Moderato

18. Thematic catalogue #18 (in G Major)/*50 Advanced Studies* #14 (in F)

C.J.W. Op. 8, No. 2

*B♮ in original edition

19. Thematic catalogue #8/*50 Advanced Studies* #21

Andante cantabile*

Ausführung: *Execution:*

C.J.W. Op. 8, No. 2

*Per CJW's thematic catalog. In 50 *Advanced Studies,* the tempo marking is "Andante Sostenuto."

20. Thematic catalogue #9/*50 Advanced Studies* #22

C.J.W. Op. 8, No. 2

21. Thematic catalogue #10/*50 Advanced Studies* #15

C.J.W. Op. 8, No. 2

22. Sight-reading and Rhythm Study: Bona *Method,* No. 77

Metodo Completo per la Divisione, Part II

23. Play Etude No. 5, Milde *Studies in Scales and Chords* (p. 146).

24. Play Etude No. 6, Milde *Studies in Scales and Chords* (p. 147).

Recommended orchestral excerpts:
- Brahms, *Violin Concerto*, Mvt. 2, Bsn 2, opening
- Tchaikovsky, *Symphony No. 4*, Mvt. 1, mm. 294-300

Lesson 3
B♭ Major and G Minor

1. B♭ Major Long Tones. Breathe as needed. C.J.W. Op. 8, No. 1/D.E.S.

vollklingend (with full tone)

Play each repeated passage three times: 1st time slurred, 2nd time legato, 3rd time staccato.

2. B♭ Major Scale C.J.W. Op. 8, No. 1/D.E.S.

3. B♭ Major Scale in Thirds

4. Tonic Major Triad (I, B♭)

5. Tonic Major Seventh Chord (I7, B♭maj7)

6. Dominant Seventh Chord (V7, F7)

7. Leading-tone Half-diminished Seventh Chord (viiø7, aø7)

8. G Minor Long Tones. Breathe as needed. C.J.W. Op. 8, No. 1/D.E.S.

9. G Natural Minor Scale

C.J.W. Op. 8, No. 1/D.E.S.

10. G Harmonic Minor Scale

C.J.W. Op. 8, No. 1/D.E.S.

11. G Melodic Minor Scale

C.J.W. Op. 8, No. 1/D.E.S.

12. Tonic Minor Triad (i, Gm)

13. Tonic Minor Seventh Chord (i⁷, Gm7)

14. Dominant Seventh Chord (V⁷, D⁷)

15. Leading-tone Fully-diminished Seventh Chord (vii°⁷, f♯°⁷)

16. Thematic catalogue #11/*50 Advanced Studies* #16

Allegro

C.J.W. Op. 8, No. 2

17. Thematic catalogue #12/*50 Advanced Studies* #8

C.J.W. Op. 8, No. 2

Allegro moderato

Etude #13 in CJW's thematic catalog (B♭ Major) was not included in the Peters 1887 edition and is now lost.

18. Thematic catalogue #14/*50 Advanced Studies* #10

C.J.W. Op. 8, No. 2

19. Thematic catalogue #15/*50 Advanced Studies* #17

C.J.W. Op. 8, No. 2

20. Thematic catalogue #37 (in F♯ minor)/*50 Advanced Studies* #23 (in G Minor)

C.J.W. Op. 8, No. 2

Poco adagio

21. Sight-reading and Rhythm Study: Bona *Method,* No. 78
(This etude was originally in cut-time. It may be practiced in two and/or in four.)

Metodo Completo per la Divisione, Part II

Allegro moderato

22. Play Etude No. 9, Milde *Studies in Scales and Chords* (p. 150).

23. Play Etude No. 10, Milde *Studies in Scales and Chords* (p. 151).

Recommended orchestral excerpts:
- Beethoven, *Violin Concerto,* Mvt. 3, mm. 134-158
- Berlioz, *Symphony Fantastique,* Mvt. 4, mm. 49-63

Lesson 4
G Major and E Minor

1. G Major Long Tones. Breathe as needed.
C.J.W. Op. 8, No. 1/D.E.S.

Sostenuto

mit vollem Ton (with full tone)

Play each repeated passage three times: 1st time slurred, 2nd time legato, 3rd time staccato.

2. G Major Scale
C.J.W. Op. 8, No. 1/D.E.S.

3. G Major Scale in Thirds

4. Tonic Major Triad (I, G)

5. Tonic Major Seventh Chord (I^7, G^{maj7})

6. Dominant Seventh Chord (V^7, D^7)

7. Leading-tone Half-diminished Seventh Chord (vii^{ø7}, f$\sharp$^{ø7})

8. E Minor Long Tones. Breathe as needed.
C.J.W. Op. 8, No. 1/D.E.S.

Sostenuto

mf < > < > *sim.*

< > < > *sim.*

9. E Natural Minor Scale

C.J.W. Op. 8, No. 1/D.E.S.

10. E Harmonic Minor Scale

C.J.W. Op. 8, No. 1/D.E.S.

11. E Melodic Minor Scale

C.J.W. Op. 8, No. 1/D.E.S.

12. Tonic Minor Triad (i, Em)

13. Tonic Minor Seventh Chord (i⁷, Em⁷)

14. Dominant Seventh Chord (V⁷, B⁷)

15. Leading-tone Fully-diminished Seventh Chord (viiº⁷, d♯º⁷)

16. Thematic catalogue #16/*50 Advanced Studies* #4

Andante sostenuto

C.J.W. Op. 8, No. 2

17. Thematic catalogue #17/*50 Advanced Studies* #18

C.J.W. Op. 8, No. 2

Allegro moderato

18. Thematic catalogue #18/*50 Advanced Studies* #14 (in F Major)

C.J.W. Op. 8, No. 2

*C♯ in original edition

19. Thematic catalogue #19/*50 Advanced Studies* #37

C.J.W. Op. 8, No. 2

20. Thematic catalogue #20/*50 Advanced Studies* #19

C.J.W. Op. 8, No. 2

21. Sight-reading and Rhythm Study: Bona *Method,* No. 79

Andantino

Metodo Completo per la Divisione, Part II

22. Play Etude No. 3, Milde *Studies in Scales and Chords* (p. 144).

23. Play Etude No. 4, Milde *Studies in Scales and Chords* (p. 145).

Recommended orchestral excerpts:
- Beethoven, *Violin Concerto,* Mvt. 2, mm. 20-30
- Tchaikovsky, *Symphony No. 5,* Mvt. 1, solos after rehearsal Q
- Tchaikovsky, *Symphony No. 6,* Mvt. 1, mm. 1-12

Lesson 5
D Major and B Minor

1. D Major Long Tones. Breathe as needed.

C.J.W. Op. 8, No. 1/D.E.S.

Sostenuto

mit vollem Ton (with full tone)

Play each repeated passage three times: 1st time slurred, 2nd time legato, 3rd time staccato.

2. D Major Scale

C.J.W. Op. 8, No. 1/D.E.S.

3. D Major Scale in Thirds

4. Tonic Major Triad (I, D)

5. Tonic Major Seventh Chord (I7, Dmaj7)

6. Dominant Seventh Chord (V7, A7)

7. Leading-tone Half-diminished Seventh Chord (viiø7, c#ø7)

8. B Minor Long Tones. Breathe as needed.

C.J.W. Op. 8, No. 1/D.E.S.

Sostenuto

dolce

9. B Natural Minor Scale

C.J.W. Op. 8, No. 1/D.E.S.

10. B Harmonic Minor Scale

C.J.W. Op. 8, No. 1/D.E.S.

11. B Melodic Minor Scale

C.J.W. Op. 8, No. 1/D.E.S.

12. Tonic Minor Triad (i, B^m)

13. Tonic Minor Seventh Chord (i^7, B^m7)

14. Dominant Seventh Chord (V^7, F♯^7)

15. Leading-tone Fully-diminished Seventh Chord (vii^o7, a♯^o7)

16. Thematic catalogue #21/*50 Advanced Studies* #27

17. Thematic catalogue #22/*50 Advanced Studies* #6 (in C Major)

C.J.W. Op. 8, No. 2

18. Thematic catalogue #23/*50 Advanced Studies* #32

C.J.W. Op. 8, No. 2

Alla marcia*

*Per CJW's thematic catalog. Tempo marking in *50 Advanced Studies* is "Tempo di Marcia."

19. Thematic catalogue #24/*50 Advanced Studies* #5

Allegro furioso

C.J.W. Op. 8, No. 2

20. Thematic catalogue #25/*50 Advanced Studies* #33

C.J.W. Op. 8, No. 2

un poco più lento

21. Sight-reading and Rhythm Study: Bona *Method,* No. 80

Metodo Completo per la Divisione, Part II

22. Play Etude No. 7, Milde *Studies in Scales and Chords* (p. 148).

23. Play Etude No. 8, Milde *Studies in Scales and Chords* (p. 149).

Recommended orchestral excerpts:
- Prokofiev, *Peter and the Wolf,* solos
- Rimsky-Korsakov, *Scheherezade,* Mvt. 2, mm. 5-26

Lesson 6
E♭ Major and C Minor

1. E♭ Major Long Tones. Breathe as needed.

C.J.W. Op. 8, No. 1/D.E.S.

Play each repeated passage three times: 1st time slurred, 2nd time legato, 3rd time staccato.

2. E♭ Major Scale

C.J.W. Op. 8, No. 1/D.E.S.

3. E♭ Major Scale in Thirds

4. Tonic Major Triad (I, E♭)

5. Tonic Major Seventh Chord (I⁷, E♭maj7)

6. Dominant Seventh Chord (V⁷, B♭⁷)

7. Leading-tone Half-diminished Seventh Chord (viiø⁷, dø⁷)

8. C Minor Long Tones. Breathe as needed.

9. C Natural Minor Scale

C.J.W. Op. 8, No. 1/D.E.S.

10. C Harmonic Minor Scale

C.J.W. Op. 8, No. 1/D.E.S.

11. C Melodic Minor Scale

C.J.W. Op. 8, No. 1/D.E.S.

12. Tonic Minor Triad (i, Cm)

13. Tonic Minor Seventh Chord (i7, Cm7)

14. Dominant Seventh Chord (V7, G7)

15. Leading-tone Fully-diminished Seventh Chord (viio7, bo7)

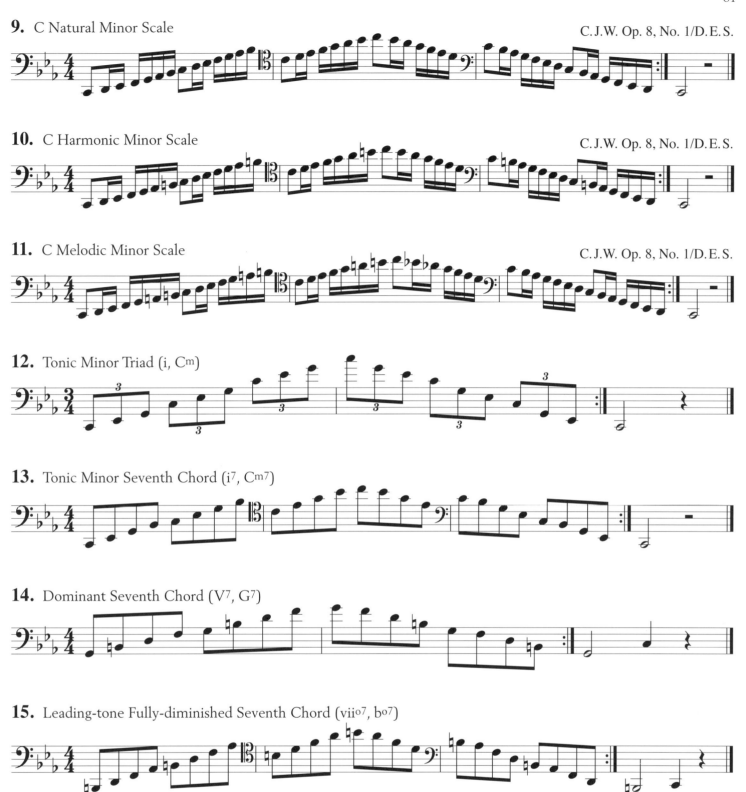

16. Thematic catalogue #26/*50 Advanced Studies* #9

C.J.W. Op. 8, No. 2

Allegro di molto

17. Thematic catalogue #27/*50 Advanced Studies* #24

C.J.W. Op. 8, No. 2

Allegro con brio

18. Thematic catalogue #28/*50 Advanced Studies* #30

C.J.W. Op. 8, No. 2

Allegro assai

Etude #29 in CJW's thematic catalog (C Minor) was not included in the Peters 1887 edition and is now lost.

19. Sight-reading and Rhythm Study: Bona *Method,* No. 81

Metodo Completo per la Divisione, Part II

Allegro moderato assai

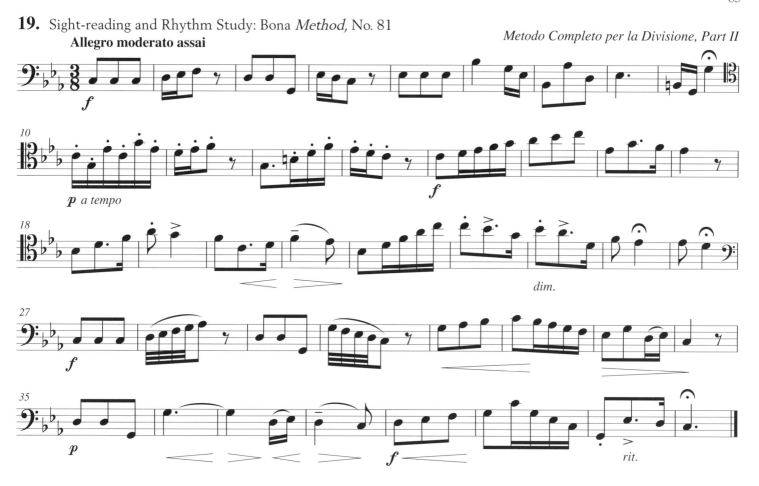

20. Play Etude No. 13, Milde *Studies in Scales and Chords* (p. 154).

21. Play Etude No. 14, Milde *Studies in Scales and Chords* (p. 155).

Recommended orchestral excerpts:
  • Beethoven, *Symphony No. 5,* Mvt. 3, mm. 268-325
  • Shostakovich, *Symphony No. 9,* Mvt. 5, mm. 1-27

Lesson 7
A♭ Major and F Minor

1. A♭ Major Long Tones. Breathe as needed.

C.J.W. Op. 8, No. 1/D.E.S.

Play each repeated passage three times: 1st time slurred, 2nd time legato, 3rd time staccato.

2. A♭ Major Scale

C.J.W. Op. 8, No. 1/D.E.S.

3. A♭ Major Scale in Thirds

4. Tonic Major Triad (I, A♭)

5. Tonic Major Seventh Chord (I⁷, A♭maj7)

6. Dominant Seventh Chord (V⁷, E♭⁷)

7. Leading-tone Half-diminished Seventh Chord (vii⊘⁷, gø⁷)

8. F Minor Long Tones. Breathe as needed.

C.J.W. Op. 8, No. 1/D.E.S.

9. F Natural Minor Scale

10. F Harmonic Minor Scale

11. F Melodic Minor Scale

12. Tonic Minor Triad (i, Fm)

13. Tonic Minor Seventh Chord (i7, Fm7)

14. Dominant Seventh Chord (V7, C7)

15. Leading-tone Fully-diminished Seventh Chord (vii°7, e°7)

16. Thematic catalogue #30/*50 Advanced Studies* #34 (in A Major)

Allegro ma non troppo*

C.J.W. Op. 8, No. 2

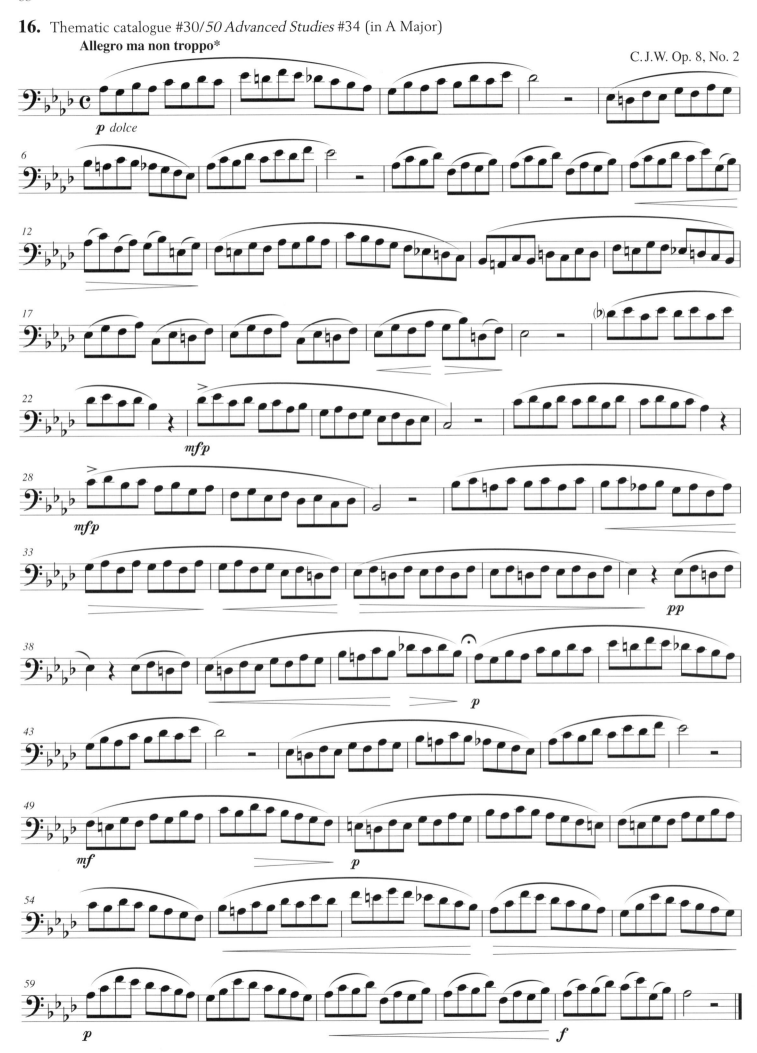

*Per CJW's thematic catalog. Tempo marking in *50 Advanced Studies* is "Andante con moto, quasi allegro moderato."

17. #31 in CJW's thematic catalog; #25 in *50 Advanced Studies*

C.J.W. Op. 8, No. 2

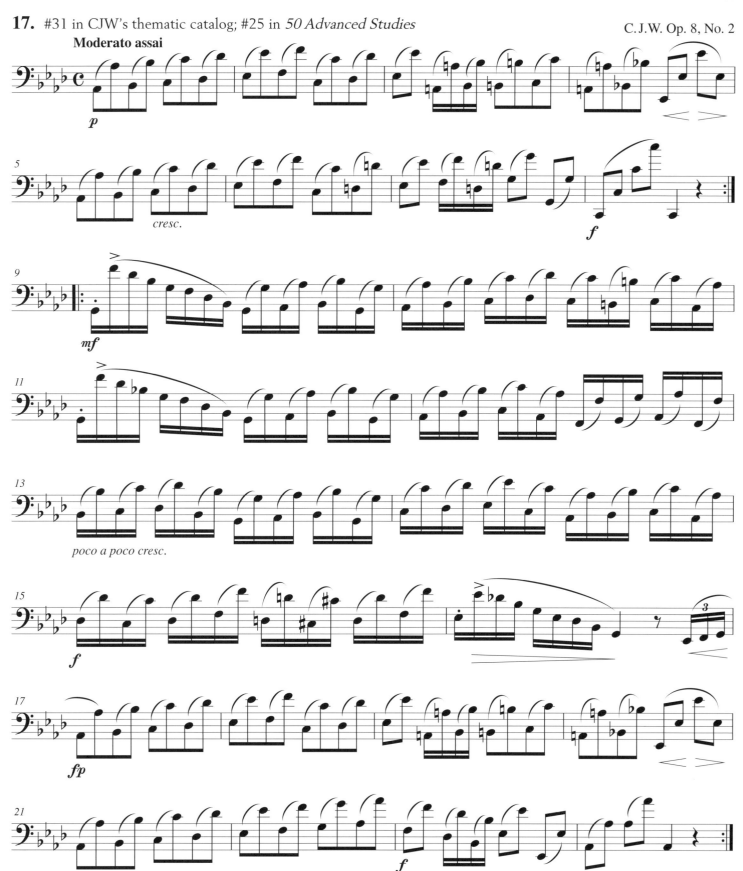

18. #32 in CJW's thematic catalog; #31 in *50 Advanced Studies*

C.J.W. Op. 8, No. 2

Andante*

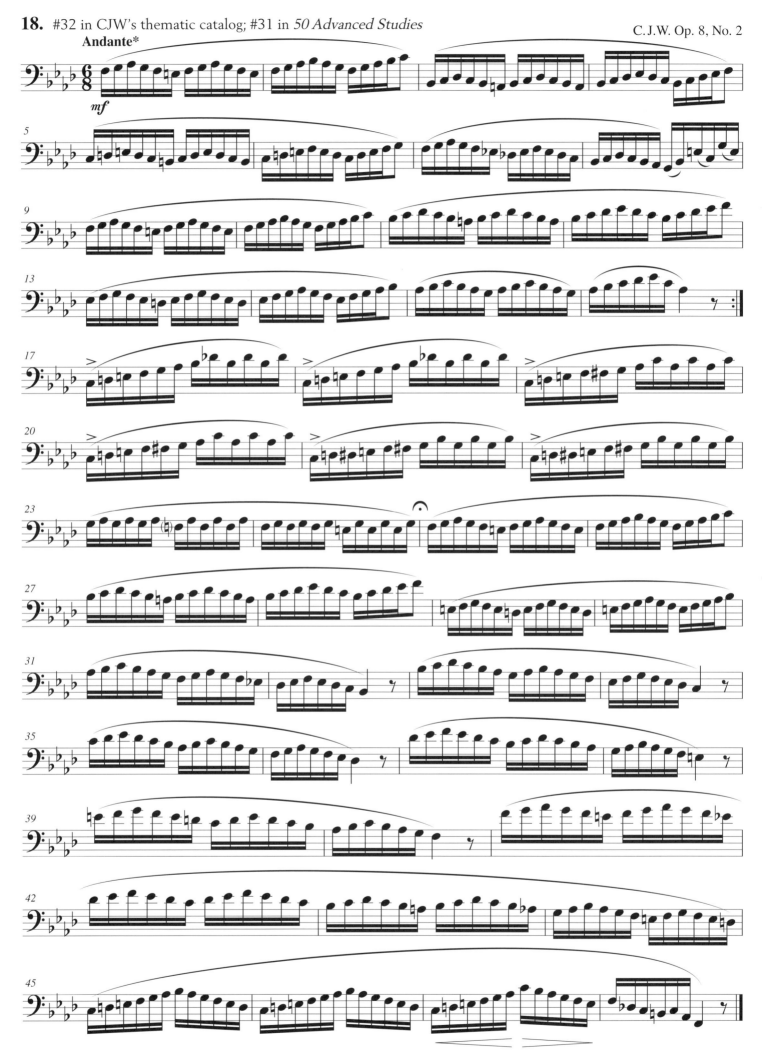

*Per CJW's thematic catalog. Tempo marking in *50 Advanced Studies* is "Andante, quasi allegretto."

Etude #33 in CJW's thematic catalog (F minor) was not included in the Peters 1887 edition and is now lost.

19. Sight-reading and Rhythm Study: Bona *Method,* No. 82

Metodo Completo per la Divisione, Part II

20. Play Etude No. 17, Milde *Studies in Scales and Chords* (p. 158).

21. Play Etude No. 18, Milde *Studies in Scales and Chords* (p. 159).

Recommended orchestral excerpts:
- Dukas, *Sorceror's Apprentice,* rehearsal 7 to rehearsal 9
- Tchaikovsky, *Symphony No. 4,* Mvt. 1, mm. 104-114

Lesson 8
A Major and F♯ Minor

New Note

C♯5 / D♭5

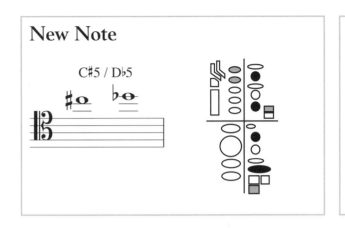

Like virtually all high notes, the resonance key (Low E♭ key) is optional on C♯5. Note the similarity between hands in this fingering (LH1 & LH3 [& LH4] / RH1 & RH3 [& RH4]).

This is one of the most difficult notes to get to speak cleanly. Experiment with venting – using the High C key, the High D key, or both – to see which combination works the best. For bassoons without a High D key, one has to rely on the High C key only; unfortunately, this may make it more difficult to get the note to speak.

Adding the A♭ key (RH4) will make the note slightly higher in pitch.

1. Introducing C♯5

2. A Major Long Tones. Breathe as needed.

C.J.W. Op. 8, No. 1/D.E.S.

mit vollem Ton (with full tone)

Play each repeated passage three times: 1st time slurred, 2nd time legato, 3rd time staccato.

3. A Major Scale

C.J.W. Op. 8, No. 1/D.E.S.

4. A Major Scale in Thirds

5. Tonic Major Triad (I, A)

6. Tonic Major Seventh Chord (I⁷, A^maj7)

7. Dominant Seventh Chord (V⁷, E⁷)

8. Leading-tone Half-diminished Seventh Chord (vii°⁷, g♯°⁷)

9. F♯ Minor Long Tones. Breathe as needed.

C.J.W. Op. 8, No. 1/D.E.S.

Sostenuto

sim.

10. F♯ Natural Minor Scale

C.J.W. Op. 8, No. 1/D.E.S.

11. F♯ Harmonic Minor Scale

C.J.W. Op. 8, No. 1/D.E.S.

12. F♯ Melodic Minor Scale

C.J.W. Op. 8, No. 1/D.E.S.

13. Tonic Minor Triad (i, F♯m)

14. Tonic Minor Seventh Chord (i⁷, F♯m⁷)

15. Dominant Seventh Chord (V⁷, C♯⁷)

16. Leading-tone Fully-diminished Seventh Chord (vii°⁷, e♯°⁷)

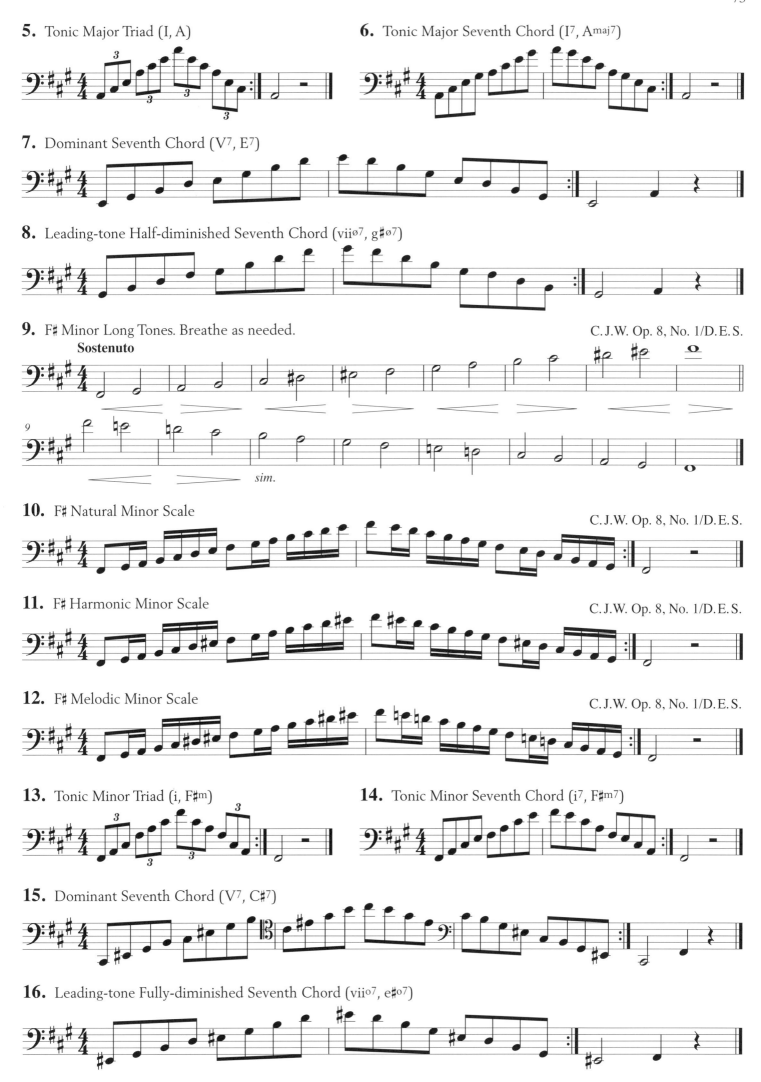

17. Thematic catalogue #30 (in A♭ Major)/*50 Advanced Studies* #34 (in A Major)

Allegro ma non troppo*

C.J.W. Op. 8, No. 2

Etudes #34 and #35 in CJW's thematic catalog (A Major) were not included in the Peters 1887 edition and are now lost.

*Per CJW's thematic catalog. Tempo marking in *50 Advanced Studies* is "Andante con moto, quasi allegro moderato."

18. Thematic catalogue #36/*50 Advanced Studies* #35

C.J.W. Op. 8, No. 2

Andante maestoso

19. Thematic catalogue #37/*50 Advanced Studies* #23 (in G minor)

C.J.W. Op. 8, No. 2

20. Sight-reading and Rhythm Study: Bona *Method,* No. 83

Metodo Completo per la Divisione, Part II

21. Play Etude No. 11, Milde *Studies in Scales and Chords* (p. 152).

22. Play Etude No. 12, Milde *Studies in Scales and Chords* (p. 153).

Recommended orchestral excerpts:
- Ravel, *Bolero,* rehearsal 2 to rehearsal 3
- Tchaikovsky, *Symphony No. 5,* Mvt. 3, rehearsal A to rehearsal E

Lesson 9
E Major and C♯ Minor

1. E Major Long Tones. Breathe as needed.

C.J.W. Op. 8, No. 1/D.E.S.

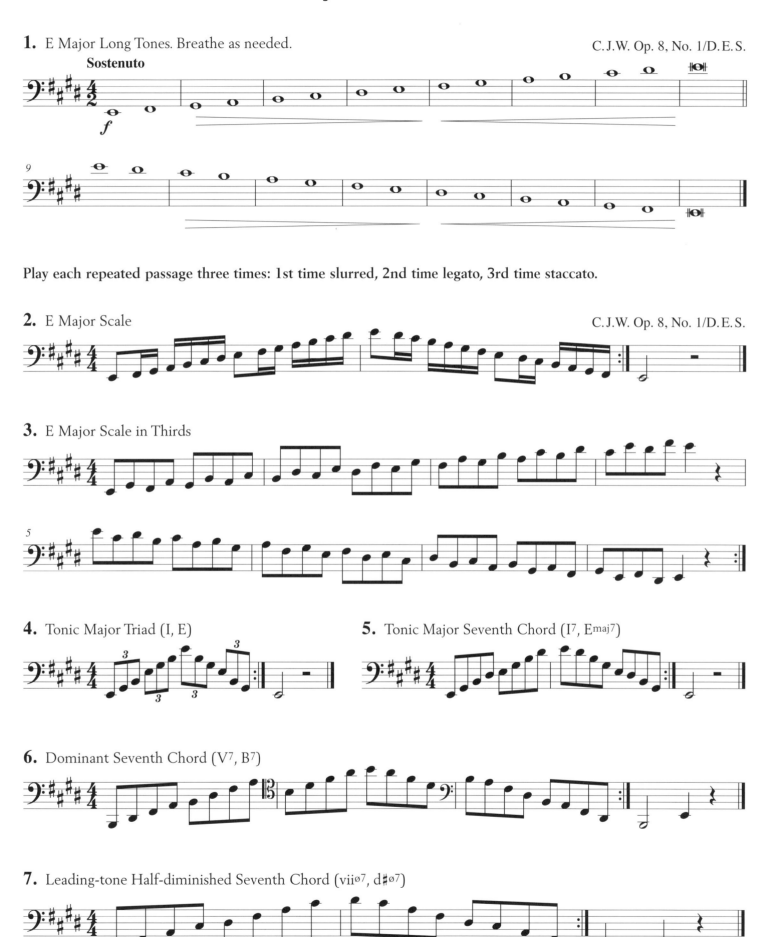

Play each repeated passage three times: 1st time slurred, 2nd time legato, 3rd time staccato.

2. E Major Scale

C.J.W. Op. 8, No. 1/D.E.S.

3. E Major Scale in Thirds

4. Tonic Major Triad (I, E)

5. Tonic Major Seventh Chord (I⁷, E^maj7)

6. Dominant Seventh Chord (V⁷, B⁷)

7. Leading-tone Half-diminished Seventh Chord (vii^ø7, d♯^ø7)

8. C# Minor Long Tones. Breathe as needed.

Sostenuto

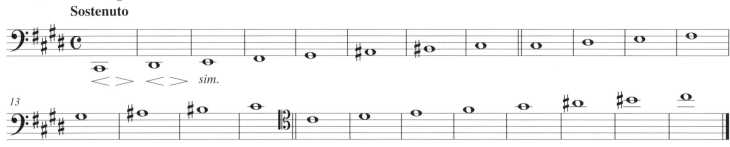

9. C# Natural Minor Scale

C.J.W. Op. 8, No. 1/D.E.S.

10. C# Harmonic Minor Scale

C.J.W. Op. 8, No. 1/D.E.S.

11. C# Melodic Minor Scale

C.J.W. Op. 8, No. 1/D.E.S.

12. Tonic Minor Triad (i, C#m)

13. Tonic Minor Seventh Chord (i⁷, C#m⁷)

14. Dominant Seventh Chord (V⁷, G#⁷)

15. Leading-tone Fully-diminished Seventh Chord (vii°⁷, b#°⁷)

16. Thematic catalogue #38/*50 Advanced Studies* #38

C.J.W. Op. 8, No. 2

17. Thematic catalogue #39/*50 Advanced Studies* #36

Allegro moderato

18. Thematic catalogue #40/*50 Advanced Studies* #39

C.J.W. Op. 8, No. 2

Etude #41 in CJW's thematic catalog (C# minor) was not included in the Peters 1887 edition and is now lost.

19. Sight-reading and Rhythm Study: Bona *Method,* No. 84

Metodo Completo per la Divisione, Part II

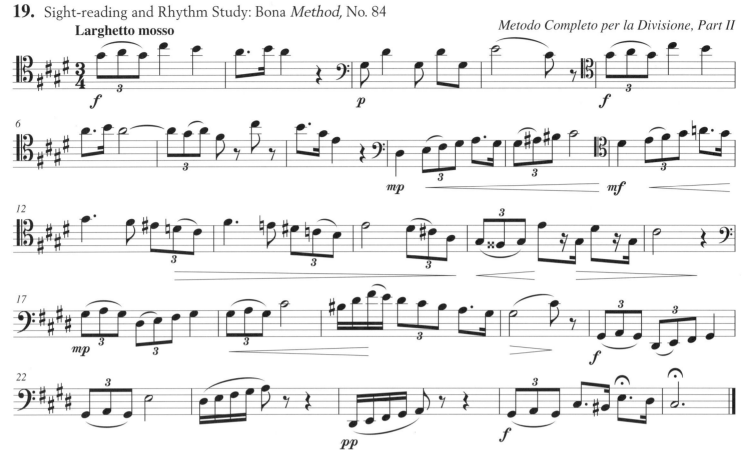

20. Play Etude No. 15, Milde *Studies in Scales and Chords* (p. 156).

21. Play Etude No. 16, Milde *Studies in Scales and Chords* (p. 157).

Recommended orchestral excerpts:
- Wagner, Overture to *Tannhäuser,* Bsn. 1 & 2, mm. 1-16

Lesson 10
D♭ Major and B♭ Minor

1. D♭ Major Long Tones. Breathe as needed.

Sostenuto

C.J.W. Op. 8, No. 1/D.E.S.

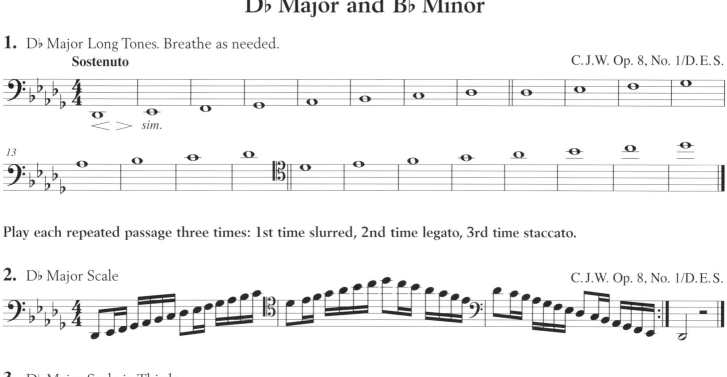

Play each repeated passage three times: 1st time slurred, 2nd time legato, 3rd time staccato.

2. D♭ Major Scale

C.J.W. Op. 8, No. 1/D.E.S.

3. D♭ Major Scale in Thirds

4. Tonic Major Triad (I, D♭)

5. Tonic Major Seventh Chord (I⁷, D♭maj7)

6. Dominant Seventh Chord (V⁷, D♭⁷)

7. Leading-tone Half-diminished Seventh Chord (viiø⁷, cø⁷)

8. B♭ Minor Long Tones. Breathe as needed.

C.J.W. Op. 8, No. 1/D.E.S.

Sostenuto

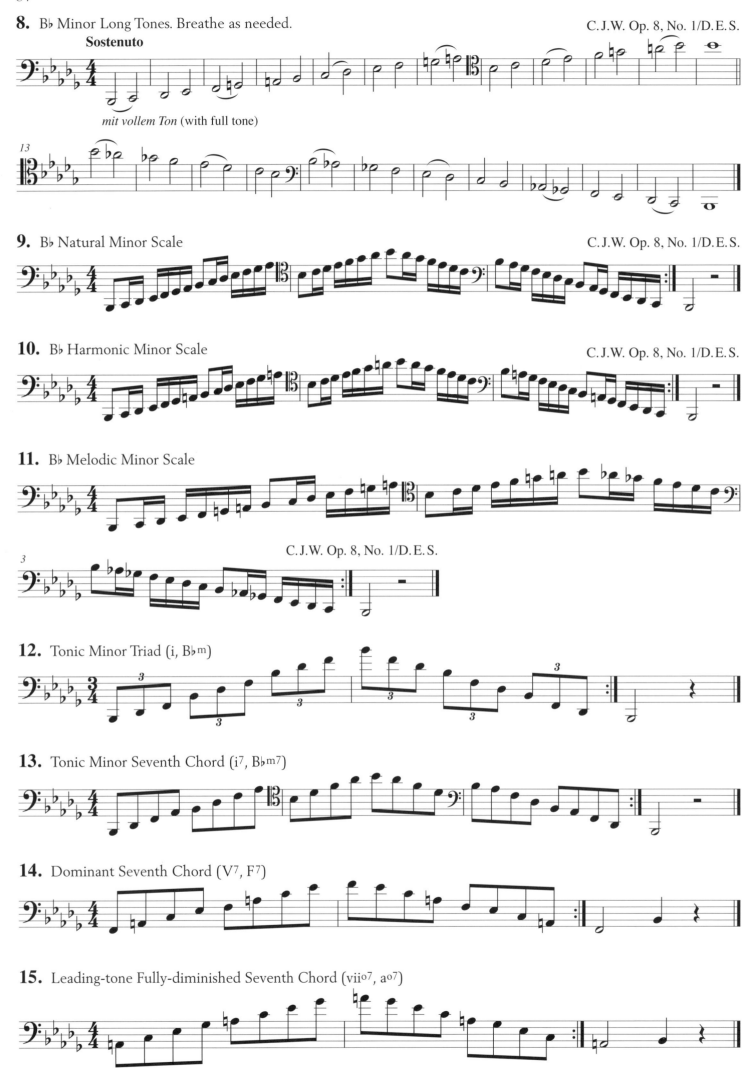

mit vollem Ton (with full tone)

9. B♭ Natural Minor Scale

C.J.W. Op. 8, No. 1/D.E.S.

10. B♭ Harmonic Minor Scale

C.J.W. Op. 8, No. 1/D.E.S.

11. B♭ Melodic Minor Scale

C.J.W. Op. 8, No. 1/D.E.S.

12. Tonic Minor Triad (i, B♭m)

13. Tonic Minor Seventh Chord (i⁷, B♭m⁷)

14. Dominant Seventh Chord (V⁷, F⁷)

15. Leading-tone Fully-diminished Seventh Chord (vii°⁷, a°⁷)

16. Thematic catalogue #52 (in C♯ Major)/*50 Advanced Studies* #40 (in D♭ Major)

C.J.W. Op. 8, No. 2

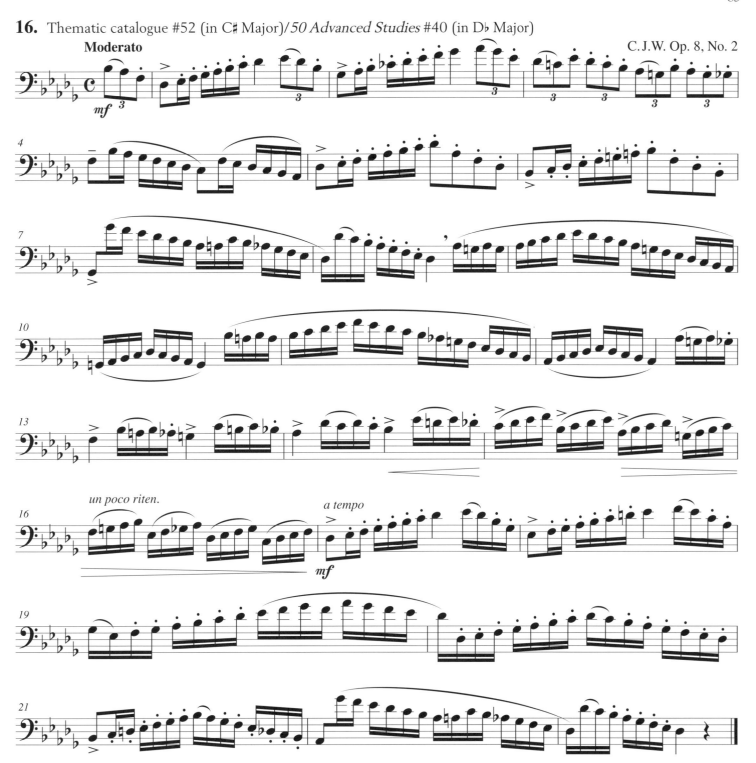

Etude #42 in CJW's thematic catalog (D♭ Major) was not included in the Peters 1887 edition and is now lost.

17. Thematic catalogue #43/*50 Advanced Studies* #41

C.J.W. Op. 8, No. 2

18. Sight-reading and Rhythm Study: Bona *Method,* No. 85

Metodo Completo per la Divisione, Part II

19. Play Etude No. 21, Milde *Studies in Scales and Chords* (p. 162).

20. Play Etude No. 22, Milde *Studies in Scales and Chords* (p. 163).

Recommended orchestral excerpts:
- Donizetti, *Una Furtiva Lagrima* from *L'Elisir d'Amore,* mm. 2-9
- Dukas, *Sorceror's Apprentice,* rehearsal 43 to rehearsal 45
- Tchaikovsky, *Symphony No. 4,* Mvt. 2, m. 274 to the end

Lesson 11
B Major and G♯ Minor

1. B Major Long Tones. Breathe as needed.

C.J.W. Op. 8, No. 1/D.E.S.

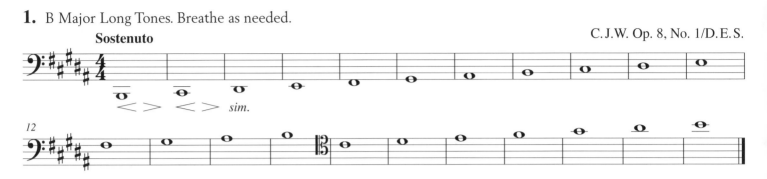

Play each repeated passage three times: 1st time slurred, 2nd time legato, 3rd time staccato.

2. B Major Scale

C.J.W. Op. 8, No. 1/D.E.S.

3. B Major Scale in Thirds

4. Tonic Major Triad (I, B)

5. Tonic Major Seventh Chord (I⁷, B maj7)

6. Dominant Seventh Chord (V⁷, F♯⁷)

7. Leading-tone Half-diminished Seventh Chord (vii∅⁷, a♯∅⁷)

8. G♯ Minor Long Tones. Breathe as needed.

C.J.W. Op. 8, No. 1/D.E.S.

9. G♯ Natural Minor Scale

C.J.W. Op. 8, No. 1/D.E.S.

10. G♯ Harmonic Minor Scale

C.J.W. Op. 8, No. 1/D.E.S.

11. G♯ Melodic Minor Scale

C.J.W. Op. 8, No. 1/D.E.S.

12. Tonic Minor Triad (i, G♯m)

13. Tonic Minor Seventh Chord (i⁷, G♯m7)

14. Dominant Seventh Chord (V⁷, D♯7)

15. Leading-tone Fully-diminished Seventh Chord (vii°⁷, f×°7)

16. Thematic catalogue #44/*50 Advanced Studies #42*

Allegro ma non troppo (alla breve)

C.J.W. Op. 8, No. 2

Etude #45 in CJW's thematic catalog was not included in the Peters 1887 edition and is now lost. As a result, there is no surviving Advanced Study in G♯ Minor. The etude below from Op. 8, No. 1 is provided as a substitute.

17.

C.J.W. Op. 8, No. 1

18. Sight-reading and Rhythm Study: Bona *Method,* No. 86

Metodo Completo per la Divisione, Part II

19. Play Etude No. 19, Milde *Studies in Scales and Chords* (p. 160).

20. Play Etude No. 20, Milde *Studies in Scales and Chords* (p. 161).

Lesson 12
G♭ Major and E♭ Minor

1. G♭ Major Long Tones. Breathe as needed.

C.J.W. Op. 8, No. 1/D.E.S.

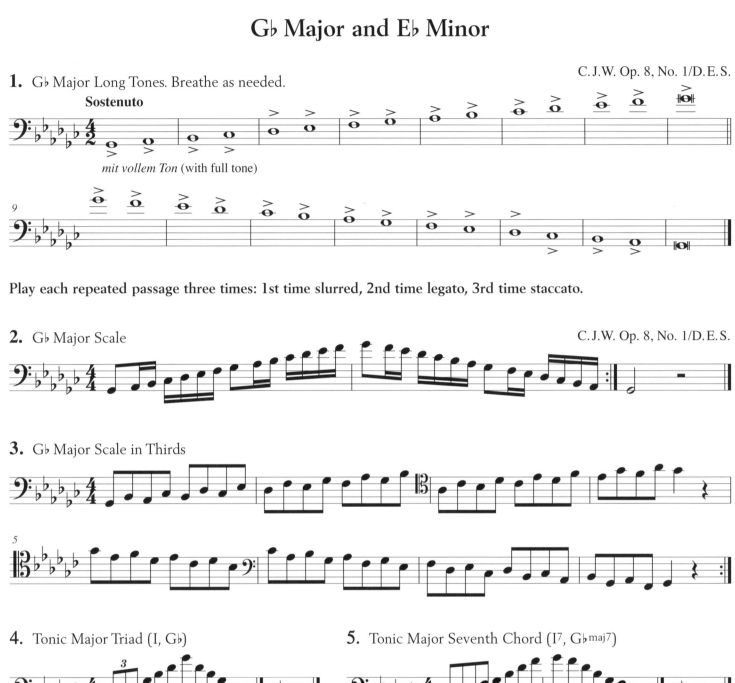

Play each repeated passage three times: 1st time slurred, 2nd time legato, 3rd time staccato.

2. G♭ Major Scale

C.J.W. Op. 8, No. 1/D.E.S.

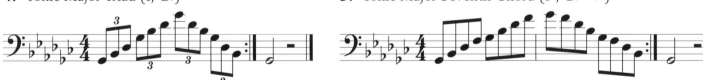

3. G♭ Major Scale in Thirds

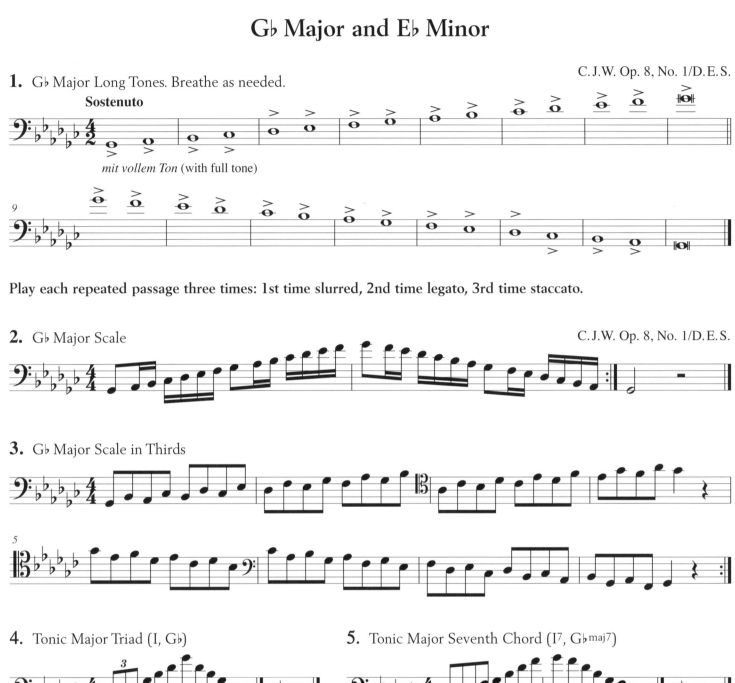

4. Tonic Major Triad (I, G♭)   **5.** Tonic Major Seventh Chord (I⁷, G♭ᵐᵃʲ⁷)

6. Dominant Seventh Chord (V⁷, D♭⁷)

7. Leading-tone Half-diminished Seventh Chord (viiø⁷, fø⁷)

8. E♭ Minor Long Tones. Breathe as needed.

C.J.W. Op. 8, No. 1/D.E.S.

9. E♭ Natural Minor Scale

C.J.W. Op. 8, No. 1/D.E.S.

10. E♭ Harmonic Minor Scale

C.J.W. Op. 8, No. 1/D.E.S.

11. E♭ Melodic Minor Scale

C.J.W. Op. 8, No. 1/D.E.S.

12. Tonic Minor Triad (i, E♭m)

13. Tonic Minor Seventh Chord (i⁷, E♭m⁷)

14. Dominant Seventh Chord (V⁷, B♭⁷)

15. Leading-tone Fully-diminished Seventh Chord (vii°⁷, d°⁷)

16. Thematic catalogue #46/*50 Advanced Studies* #44

Tema con variazioni

Andante. Intrada

C.J.W. Op. 8, No. 2

17. Thematic catalogue #47/*50 Advanced Studies* #45

18. Sight-reading and Rhythm Study: Bona *Method,* No. 87

Metodo Completo per la Divisione, Part II

Moderato assai

19. Play Etude No. 24A, Milde *Studies in Scales and Chords* (p. 166).

20. Play Etude No. 24B, Milde *Studies in Scales and Chords* (p. 167).

Recommended orchestral excerpts:
- Stravinsky, *Berceuse* from *The Firebird,* rehearsal 183 to rehearsal 187

Lesson 13
F♯ Major and D♯ Minor

1. F♯ Major Long Tones. Breathe as needed.

C.J.W. Op. 8, No. 1/D.E.S.

mit vollem Ton (with full tone)

Play each repeated passage three times: 1st time slurred, 2nd time legato, 3rd time staccato.

2. F♯ Major Scale

C.J.W. Op. 8, No. 1/D.E.S.

3. F♯ Major Scale in Thirds

4. Tonic Major Triad (I, F♯)

5. Tonic Major Seventh Chord (I⁷, F♯ᵐᵃʲ⁷)

6. Dominant Seventh Chord (V⁷, C♯⁷)

7. Leading-tone Half-diminished Seventh Chord (vii°⁷, e♯°⁷)

8. D♯ Minor Long Tones. Breathe as needed.

C.J.W. Op. 8, No. 1/D.E.S.

dolce

9. D♯ Natural Minor Scale

C.J.W. Op. 8, No. 1/D.E.S.

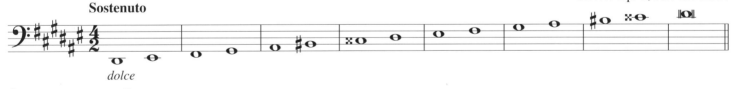

10. D♯ Harmonic Minor Scale

C.J.W. Op. 8, No. 1/D.E.S.

11. D♯ Melodic Minor Scale

C.J.W. Op. 8, No. 1/D.E.S.

12. Tonic Minor Triad (i, D♯m)

13. Tonic Minor Seventh Chord (i⁷, D♯m⁷)

14. Dominant Seventh Chord (V⁷, A♯⁷)

15. Leading-tone Fully-diminished Seventh Chord (vii°⁷, c×°⁷)

Etude #48 in CJW's thematic catalog was not included in the Peters 1887 edition and is now lost. As a result, there is no surviving Advanced Study in F♯ Major. The etude below from Op. 8, No. 1 is provided as a substitute.

16. **Alla marcia**

C.J.W. Op. 8, No. 1/D.E.S.

17. Thematic catalogue #49/*50 Advanced Studies* #43

C.J.W. Op. 8, No. 2

Adagio, ma non strasciando

18. Sight-reading and Rhythm Study: Bona *Method,* No. 88

Metodo Completo per la Divisione, Part II

19. Play Etude No. 23, Milde *Studies in Scales and Chords* (p. 164).

20. Play Etude No. 24, Milde *Studies in Scales and Chords* (p. 165).

Recommended orchestral excerpts:
- Beethoven, *Symphony No. 4,* Mvt. 2

Lesson 14
C♭ Major and A♭ Minor

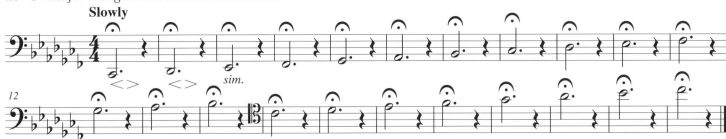

1. C♭ Major Long Tones. Breathe as needed.

Play each repeated passage three times: 1st time slurred, 2nd time legato, 3rd time staccato.

2. C♭ Major Scale   C.J.W. Op. 8, No. 1/D.E.S.

3. C♭ Major Scale in Thirds

4. Tonic Major Triad (I, C♭)

5. Tonic Major Seventh Chord (I^7, C♭^{maj7})

6. Dominant Seventh Chord (V^7, G♭^{7})

7. Leading-tone Half-diminished Seventh Chord (vii^{ø7}, b♭^{ø7})

8. A♭ Minor Long Tones. Breathe as needed.

9. A♭ Natural Minor Scale   C.J.W. Op. 8, No. 1/D.E.S.

10. A♭ Harmonic Minor Scale

C.J.W. Op. 8, No. 1/D.E.S.

11. A♭ Melodic Minor Scale

C.J.W. Op. 8, No. 1/D.E.S.

12. Tonic Minor Triad (i, A♭m)

13. Tonic Minor Seventh Chord (i⁷, A♭m⁷)

14. Dominant Seventh Chord (V⁷, E♭⁷)

15. Leading-tone Fully-diminished Seventh Chord (vii°⁷, g°⁷)

16. Thematic catalogue #50/*50 Advanced Studies* #46

C.J.W. Op. 8, No. 2

Andante con moto, quasi allegretto

17. Thematic catalogue #51/*50 Advanced Studies* #47

C.J.W. Op. 8, No. 2

Andante con moto

18. Sight-reading and Rhythm Study: Bona *Method,* No. 89

Sostenuto

Metodo Completo per la Divisione, Part II

19. Play Etude No. 24E, Milde *Studies in Scales and Chords* (p. 170).

20. Play Etude No. 24F, Milde *Studies in Scales and Chords* (p. 171).

Recommended orchestral excerpts:
- Stravinsky, *Rite of Spring,* rehearsal 12

Lesson 15
C♯ Major and A♯ Minor

1. C♯ Major Long Tones. Breathe as needed.

Play each repeated passage three times: 1st time slurred, 2nd time legato, 3rd time staccato.

2. C♯ Major Scale

C.J.W. Op. 8, No. 1/D.E.S.

3. C♯ Major Scale in Thirds

4. Tonic Major Triad (I, C♯)

5. Tonic Major Seventh Chord (I⁷, C♯maj7)

6. Dominant Seventh Chord (V⁷, G♯⁷)

7. Leading-tone Half-diminished Seventh Chord (vii⁰⁷, b#ᵒ⁷)

8. A# Minor Long Tones. Breathe as needed.

9. A# Natural Minor Scale

C.J.W. Op. 8, No. 1/D.E.S.

10. A# Harmonic Minor Scale

C.J.W. Op. 8, No. 1/D.E.S.

11. A# Melodic Minor Scale

C.J.W. Op. 8, No. 1/D.E.S.

12. Tonic Minor Triad (i, A#m)

13. Tonic Minor Seventh Chord (i⁷, A#m⁷)

14. Dominant Seventh Chord (V⁷, E#⁷)

15. Leading-tone Fully-diminished Seventh Chord (vii°⁷, g𝄪ᵒ⁷)

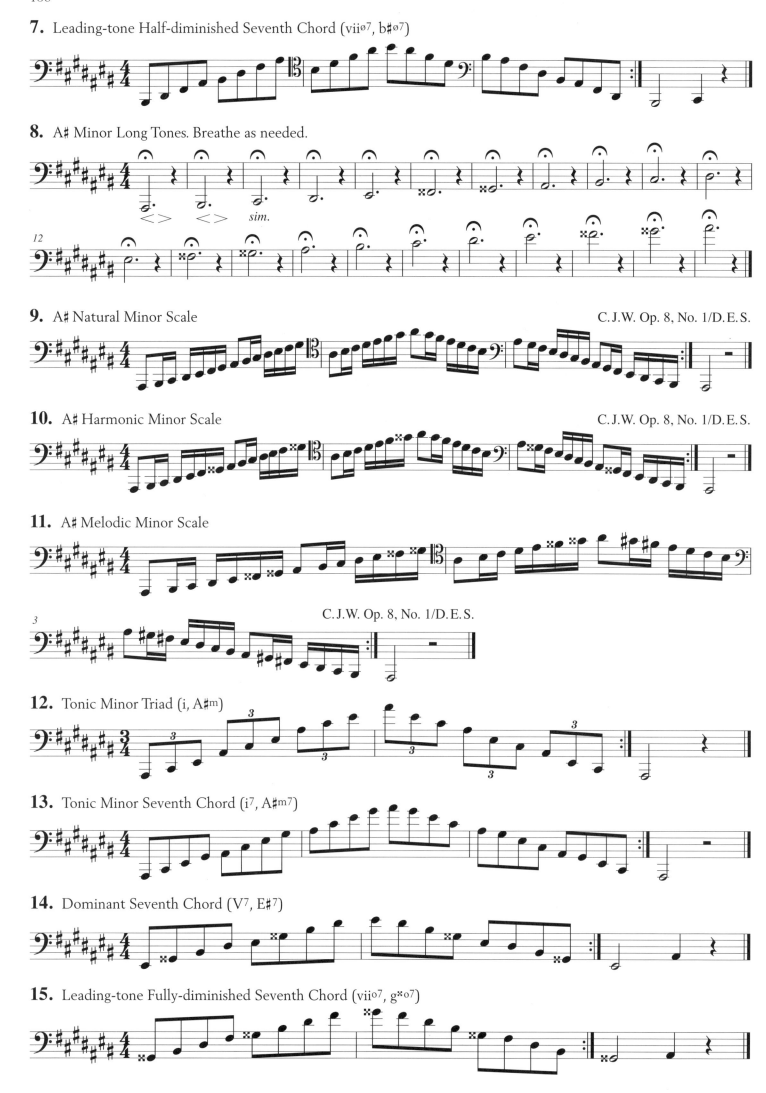

16. Thematic catalogue #52 (in C♯ Major)/*50 Advanced Studies* #40 (in D♭ Major)

C.J.W. Op. 8, No. 2

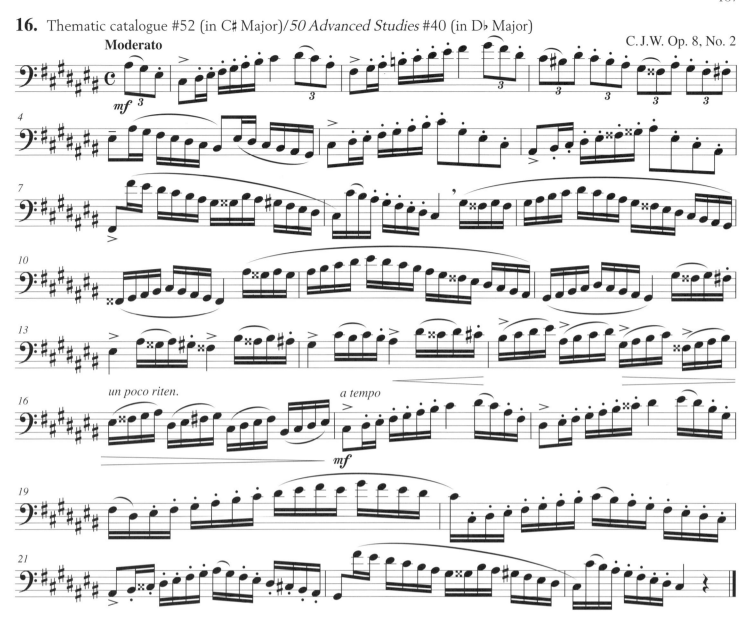

Etude #53 in CJW's thematic catalog was not included in the Peters 1887 edition and is now lost. As a result, there is no surviving Advanced Study in A♯ Minor. The etude below from Op. 8, No. 1 is provided as a substitute.

17. Andante con moto

C.J.W. Op. 8, No. 1/D.E.S.

zart, aber ausdrucksvoll (delicately, but with expression)

18. Sight-reading and Rhythm Study: Bona *Method,* No. 90

Metodo Completo per la Divisione, Part II

19. Play Etude No. 24C, Milde *Studies in Scales and Chords* (p. 168).

20. Play Etude No. 24D, Milde *Studies in Scales and Chords* (p. 169).

VIRTUOSITY STUDIES

Lesson 16
Chromatic Scales

1. Chromatic Scale Long Tones. Breathe as needed.

Slowly

C.J.W. Op. 8, No. 1/D.E.S.

2. Review chromatic scales on B♭ Major from "Review" (p. 20, #2 and #3).

3. Review Etude No. 25A, Milde *Studies in Scales and Chords* (p. 174).

Play each repeated passage three times: 1st time slurred, 2nd time legato, 3rd time staccato.

4. Chromatic Scale in Triplets on B♮

5. Chromatic Scale in Sixteenths on B♮

6. Play Etude No. 25B, Milde *Studies in Scales and Chords* (p. 176).

7. Chromatic Scale in Triplets on C♮

8. Chromatic Scale in Sixteenths on C♮

9. Play Etude No. 25, Milde *Studies in Scales and Chords* (p. 172).

10. Chromatic Scale in Triplets on D♭

11. Chromatic Scale in Sixteenths on D♭

12. Play Etude No. 25C, Milde *Studies in Scales and Chords* (p. 178).

13. Thematic catalogue #54 (in C Major)/*50 Advanced Studies* #20 (in B♭ Major)

C.J.W. Op. 8, No. 2

14. Sight-reading and Rhythm Study: Bona *Method,* No. 91

Metodo Completo per la Divisione, Part II

Lesson 17
Miscellaneous Virtuosity Studies

1. Thematic catalogue #55/*50 Advanced Studies* #28

Scherzo

Allegro vivace

C.J.W. Op. 8, No. 2

2. Thematic catalogue #56/*50 Advanced Studies* #11

Vivace

C.J.W. Op. 8, No. 2

Siehe B-dur-Sinfonie von Robert Schumann
See: Symphony in B♭ major by Robert Schumann

Lebhaft *(Lively)*

3. Sight-reading and Rhythm Study: Bona *Method,* No. 92

Metodo Completo per la Divisione, Part II

Andante

4. Sight-reading and Rhythm Study: Bona *Method,* No. 93

Metodo Completo per la Divisione, Part II

5. Sight-reading and Rhythm Study: Bona *Method,* No. 94

Metodo Completo per la Divisione, Part II

6. Sight-reading and Rhythm Study: Bona *Method,* No. 95

Metodo Completo per la Divisione, Part II

Recommended orchestral excerpts:
- Bartok, *Concerto for Orchestra,* Mvt. 2, bassoon duet and trio (all parts)
- Ravel, *Piano Concerto in G,* Mvt. 3, Bsn. 1 & 2, rehearsal 14 to rehearsal 16
- Ravel, *Rapsodie Espagnole,* Bsn. 1 & 2, rehearsal 8 to rehearsal 9
- Rimsky-Korsakov, *Scheherezade,* Mvt. 2, cadenzas
- Schumann, *Symphony No. 1,* Mvt. 1, solo after rehearsal B
- Strauss, *Till Eulenspiegels Lustige Streiche,* 6 before rehearsal 32 to 8 after rehearsal 33

118

Lesson 18
D5

New Note

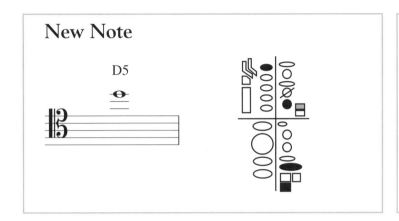

D5

Like virtually all high notes, the resonance key (Low E♭ key) is optional on D5. Note the similarity between hands if it is employed (LH3 & LH4 / RH3 & RH4). Half-holing LH2 can help D5 to speak cleanly. Experiment with the precise position of LH2 to find the optimal size of the half-hole.

For bassoons without a High D key, substitute the High C key. (Unfortunately, this will make it more difficult to get the note to speak.)

1. Introducing D5
Slowly

Play each repeated passage three times: 1st time slurred, 2nd time legato, 3rd time staccato.

2. Chromatic Scale in Triplets on D

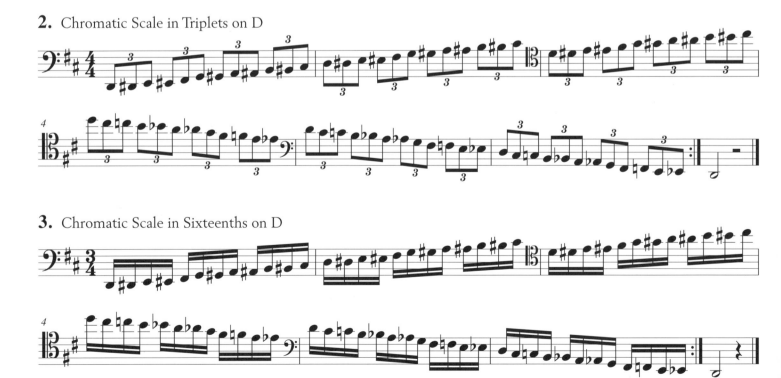

3. Chromatic Scale in Sixteenths on D

4. D Major Scale

5. Tonic Major Triad (I, D)

6. Dominant Seventh Chord (V⁷, Dmaj7)

7. D Natural Minor Scale

8. D Harmonic Minor Scale

9. D Melodic Minor Scale

10. Tonic Minor Triad (i, Dm)

11. Tonic Minor Seventh Chord (i⁷, Dm7)

12. Thematic catalogue #57/*50 Advanced Studies* #48

Andante con moto

C.J.W. Op. 8, No. 2

13. Sight-reading and Rhythm Study: Bona *Method,* No. 96

Metodo Completo per la Divisione, Part II

Allegretto moderato assai

Recommended orchestral excerpts:
- Shostakovich, *Symphony No. 9,* Mvt. 4
- Stravinsky, *Rite of Spring,* mm. 1-15

Lesson 19
D♯5 / E♭5

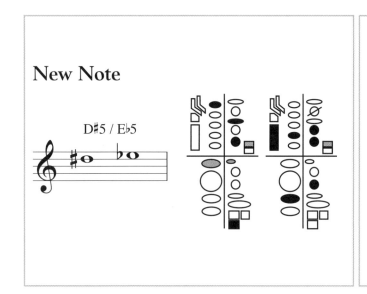

New Note

D♯5 / E♭5

Like virtually all high notes, the resonance key (Low E♭ key) is optional on E♭5.

The first fingering shown is usually the easiest technically, especially when approaching from D5, but it can be difficult to make the note speak cleanly in other situations. It also tends to be flat. Adding the B♭ Key (RH thumb) and/or the alternate C♯ trill key (RH1) can help bring the note up to pitch.

The second fingering usually speaks well and is relatively well in tune, but can be awkward technically. LH1 can be half-holed or open.

For bassoons without a High D key, the second fingering is recommended. (Substituting the High C key for the High D key likely won't work well.)

Bassoonists often use a special reed and/or bocal to play this high in the register.

1. Introducing D♯5/E♭5
Slowly

Play each repeated passage three times: 1st time slurred, 2nd time legato, 3rd time staccato.

2. Chromatic Scale in Triplets on E♭

3. Chromatic Scale in Sixteenths on E♭

4. E♭ Major Scale

5. Tonic Major Triad (I, E♭)

6. Tonic Major Seventh Chord (I⁷, E♭maj7)

7. E♭ Natural Minor Scale

8. E♭ Harmonic Minor Scale

9. E♭ Melodic Minor Scale

10. Tonic Minor Triad (i, E♭m)

11. Tonic Minor Seventh Chord (i⁷, E♭m7)

(This page intentionally blank)

12. Thematic catalogue #58/*50 Advanced Studies* #49

Andante sostenuto

C.J.W. Op. 8, No. 2

13. Thematic catalogue #59/*50 Advanced Studies* #29

C.J.W. Op. 8, No. 2

Allegro con fuoco

(This page intentionally blank)

14. Sight-reading and Rhythm Study: Bona *Method,* No. 97

Metodo Completo per la Divisione, Part II

Adagio

Lesson 20
E5

New Note

E5

Like virtually all high notes, the resonance key (Low E♭ key) is optional on E5.

The first fingering shown is usually the easiest technically, especially when approaching from a step or half-step below, but it can be difficult to make the note speak cleanly in other situations. It also tends to be flat. Adding the B♭ Key (RH thumb) and/or the alternate C♯ trill key (RH1) can help bring the note up to pitch. Note that the High E Key automatically depresses the High E♭ key.

The second fingering usually speaks well and is relatively well in tune, but can be awkward technically.

For bassoons without a High D key, the second fingering is recommended. (Substituting the High C key for the High D key likely won't work well.) The last fingering is typically used only on bassoons without a High E key.

Bassoonists often use a special reed and/or bocal to play this high in the register.

1. Introducing E5

Play each repeated passage three times: 1st time slurred, 2nd time legato, 3rd time staccato.

2. Chromatic Scale in Triplets on E

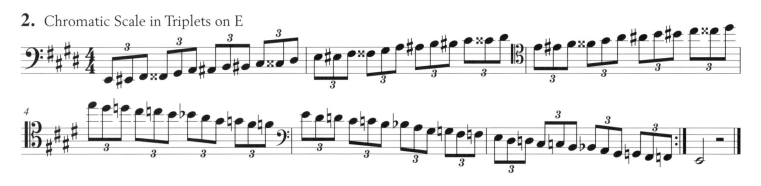

3. Chromatic Scale in Sixteenths on E

4. E Major Scale

5. Tonic Major Triad (I, E)

6. Tonic Major Seventh Chord (I⁷, E^maj7)

7. E Natural Minor Scale

8. E Harmonic Minor Scale

9. E Melodic Minor Scale

10. Tonic Minor Triad (i, E^m)

11. Tonic Minor Seventh Chord (i⁷, E^m7)

12. Thematic catalogue #60/*50 Advanced Studies* #50

Adagio di molto

13. Sight-reading and Rhythm Study: Bona *Method,* No. 98

Metodo Completo per la Divisione, Part II

Allegro moderato

Recommended orchestral excerpts:
- Ravel, *Piano Concerto in G,* Mvt. 1, rehearsal 9 to rehearsal 10

Lesson 21
Double-Tonguing

> Most advanced bassoonists learn to double-tongue at some point. Double-tonguing is used to increase tonguing speed. In short, it is a technique whereby the bassoonist alternates "Ta" and "Ka" syllables (compared to single-tonguing, which is a repetition of the "Ta" syllable only).
>
> The key to a good double-tongue is getting the "Ta" and "Ka" syllables to sound alike; that is, to get them to match in pitch, dynamic, quality of articulation, etc. Therefore, to establish a good double tongue, first work on getting these two syllables to match as closely as possible. Begin with a reed that speaks well and with a comfortable note. I suggest Bb3 or B3, holding the speaker key open the whole time. If possible, record yourself and listen back to the recording – double-tonguing will always sound different to the listener than to the bassoonist. The goal is to reach a point where a listener (including you listening to a recording of yourself) can't tell the difference between the "Ta" and "Ka" syllable.
>
> Begin wiih a comfortable tempo – neither too fast nor too slow. Also be sure to play with good air support and with full tone. Lastly, stay in a comfortable tessitura initially (I suggest C3–F4) and expand outwards from there.

Practice each measure of Exercise #1 separately, striving to get the "Ta" and "Ka" to match as closely as possible. Choose any comfortable note (hold down the speaker key if playing Bb3 as shown) and any comfortable tempo.

1. Establishing Double-Tongue

Use the measures of Exercise #2 to test that the "Ta" and "Ka" match as best as possible. Use the first measure to establish a good model, then strive to have all measures sound like that model. When a listener cannot tell a difference between the various measures, then you can be assured the syllables match well. Choose any comfortable note (hold down the speaker key if playing Bb3 as shown) and a comfortable tempo.

2. Testing Double-Tongue

J.B. Arban, *Method for the Cornet*

3.

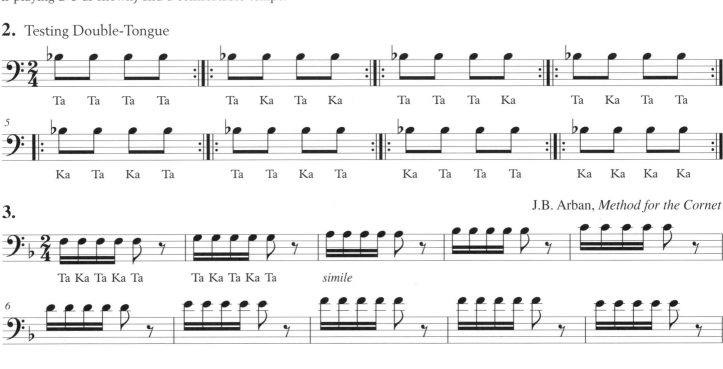

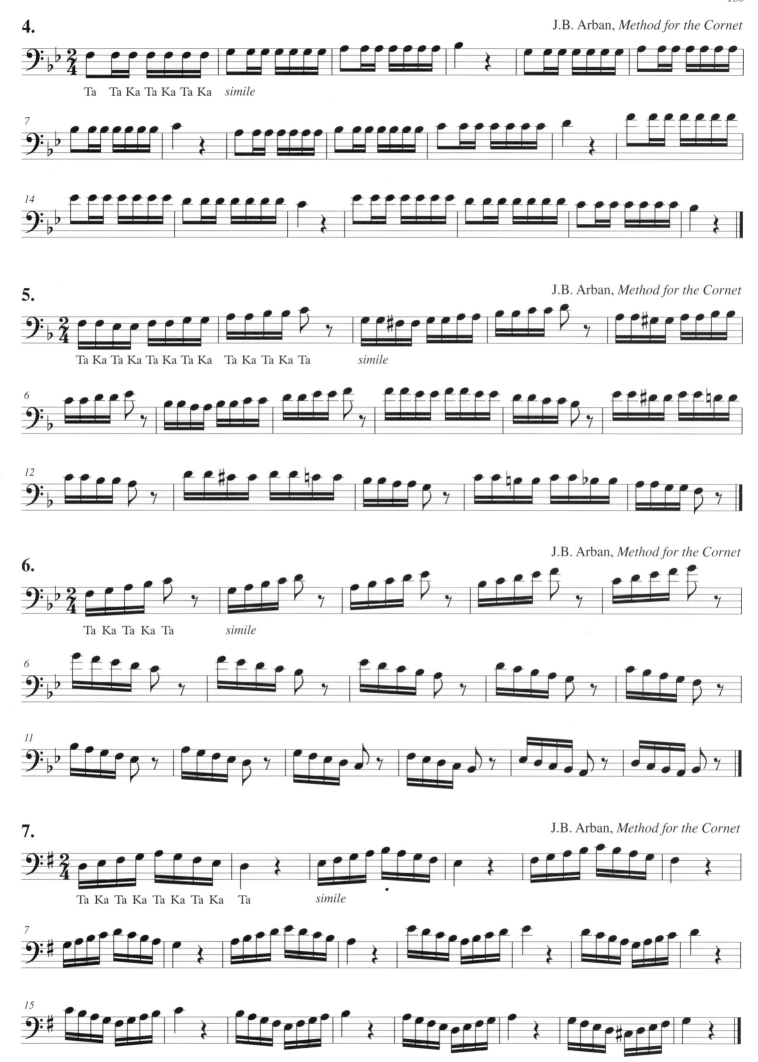

8.

J.B. Arban, *Method for the Cornet*

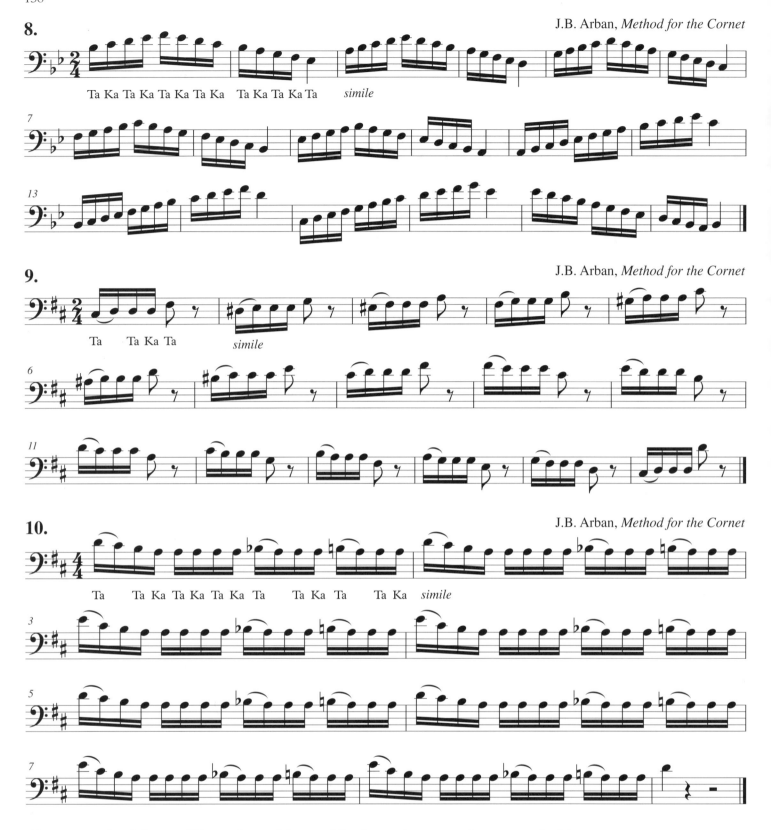

Ta Ka Ta Ka Ta Ka Ta Ka   Ta Ka Ta Ka Ta   *simile*

9.

J.B. Arban, *Method for the Cornet*

Ta   Ta Ka Ta   *simile*

10.

J.B. Arban, *Method for the Cornet*

Ta   Ta Ka Ta Ka Ta Ka Ta   Ta Ka Ta   Ta Ka   *simile*

Also re-visit the following Weissenborn *Advanced Studies* and practice them using double-tonguing:
- #6 (F Major, Lesson 2, Exercise 16 - p. 33)
- #12 (B♭ Major, Lesson 3, Exercise 17 - p. 41)
- #24 (B Minor, Lesson 5, Exercise 19 - p. 57)
- #46 - Variation 3 (G♭ Major, Lesson 12, Exercise 16 - p. 95)
- #59 (E♭ Major, Lesson 19, Exercise 13 - p. 126)

Recommended orchestral excerpts:
- Beethoven, *Symphony No. 4,* Mvt. 4, 16th note passages
- Berlioz, *Symphonie Fantastique,* Mvt. 5, mm. 47-64
- Mozart, Overture to *Marriage of Figaro*
- Mendelssohn, *Scherzo* from *A Midsummer Night's Dream,* mm. 1-26
- Smetana, Overture to *The Bartered Bride*

Lesson 22
Triple-Tonguing

Triple-tonguing is very similar to double-tonguing. It involves using both "Ta" and "Ka" syllables; however, instead of alternating these two syllables, a pattern of three syllables is employed – either "Ta-Ta-Ka" or "Ta-Ka-Ta". This is almost always done with triplet rhythms.

It should be noted that in Arban's *Method* he mentions only "Ta-Ta-Ka" (or "Tu-Tu-Ku" as he says). It should also be noted that he begins with triple-tonguing first and then progresses to double-tonguing.

Lastly, it is possible to employ double-tonguing even with triplet rhythms, as in the fourth measure of Exercise 1 below. This is a useful technique that many players use and many teachers suggest. In using this technique, make sure that the "Ka" syllables all match; beware of inadvertently over-accenting the "Ka" on beat two.

Use Exercise 1 below to establish triple-tonguing while still making sure that the "Ta" and "Ka" match as closely as possible. Use the first measure to establish a good model, then strive to have all measures sound like that model. Choose any comfortable note (hold down the speaker key if playing B♭3 as shown) and a comfortable tempo. It is best to master all of the tonguing patterns below so that you may employ any of them based upon the musical and technical demands of a passage.

1. Establishing Triple-Tongue

Ta Ta Ta Ta Ta Ta   Ta Ta Ka Ta Ta Ka   Ta Ka Ta Ta Ka Ta   Ta Ka Ta Ka Ta Ka

Practice the exercises below using the two triple-tonguing patterns ("Ta-Ta-Ka" and "Ta-Ka-Ta") as well as double-tonguing the triplets ("Ta-Ka-Ta, Ka-Ta-Ka"). Strive to master all three and develop the ability to choose which one will work best in a given situation.

2.
J.B. Arban, *Method for the Cornet*

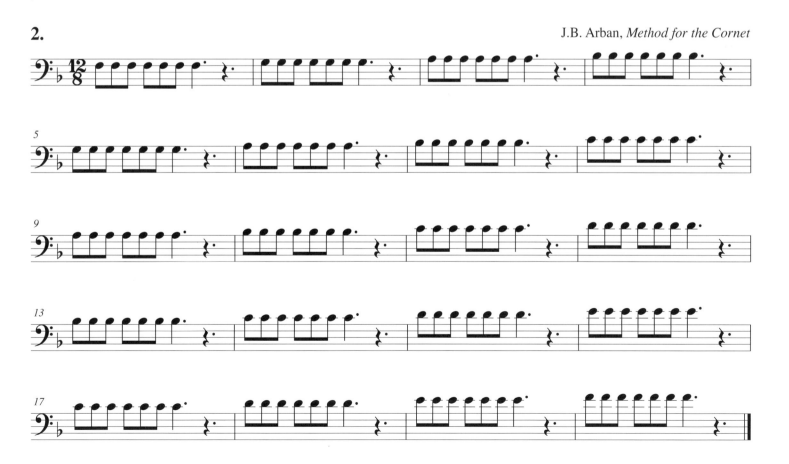

3.

J.B. Arban, *Method for the Cornet*

4.

J.B. Arban, *Method for the Cornet*

5.

J.B. Arban, *Method for the Cornet*

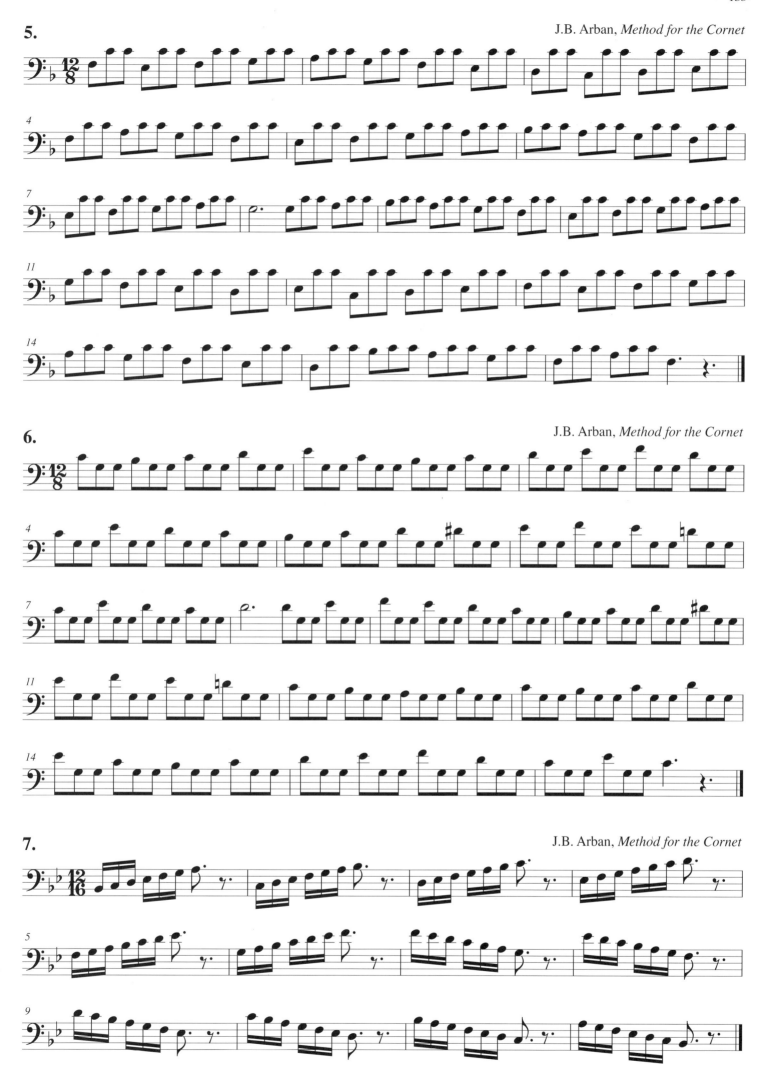

6.

J.B. Arban, *Method for the Cornet*

7.

J.B. Arban, *Method for the Cornet*

8.   J.B. Arban, *Method for the Cornet*

9.   J.B. Arban, *Method for the Cornet*

10.   J.B. Arban, *Method for the Cornet*

Also re-visit the following Weissenborn *Advanced Studies* and practice them using triple-tonguing:
- #7 (F Major, Lesson 2, Exercise 17 - p. 33)
- #9 (D Minor, Lesson 2, Exercise 20 - p. 36)

Recommended orchestral excerpts:
- Mendelssohn, *Symphony No. 4,* Bsn 1 & 2, Mvt. 1 & 4
- Ravel, *Bolero,* Bsn 1 & 2, Reh. 4-5

SUPPLEMENT

Studies on Scales and Chords, Op. 24
Ludwig Milde (1849–1913)

Nº 1

Ludwig Milde, Op. 24
Ed. by Douglas E. Spaniol

Most editions of these etudes have errors and ambiguities regarding accidentals and the octaves to which they apply. In this edition, accidentals apply only to the octave in which they appear. For the sake of clarity, courtesy accidentals are often provided to cancel accidentals from a different octave. Courtesy accidentals are not provided after clef changes. Accidentals appearing in brackets indicate that it is unclear which note Milde intended; the accidental in brackets is the editor's suggestion. Slurs added by the editor are dashed; grace notes added by the editor are in brackets.

№ 2

L. M. Op. 24/D. E. S.

*The original edition had a slur over beats 3 and 4 *and* a slur over beat 4 only, both of which appear to be errors. The editor suggests slur two – tongue two as indicated. Some editions have C for the penultimate note, but most have D; the D appears to be correct.

Nº 3

L. M. Op. 24/D. E. S.

Nº 4

L. M. Op. 24/D.E.S.

№ 5

L. M. Op. 24/D.E.S.

№ 6

L. M. Op. 24/D.E.S.

№ 7

L. M. Op. 24/D.E.S.

№ 8

L. M. Op. 24/D.E.S.

№ 9

L. M. Op. 24/D. E. S.

№ 10

L. M. Op. 24/D. E. S.

№ 11

L. M. Op. 24/D. E. S.

*This dashed slur is in the original, but appears to be an error; the solid slurs are believed to be correct.

№ 12

L. M. Op. 24/D. E. S.

Nº 13

L. M. Op. 24/D.E.S.

№ 14

L. M. Op. 24/D.E.S.

№ 15

L. M. Op. 24/D. E. S.

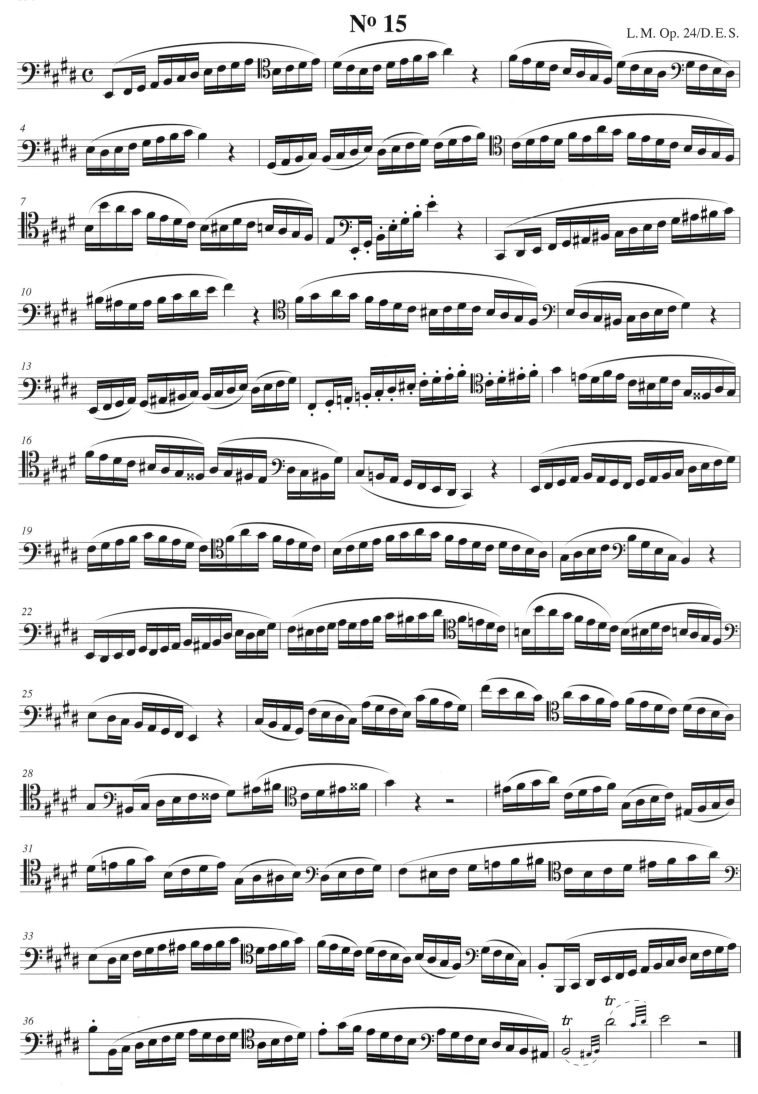

№ 16

L. M. Op. 24/D.E.S.

№ 17

L. M. Op. 24/D. E. S.

№ 18

L. M. Op. 24/D. E. S.

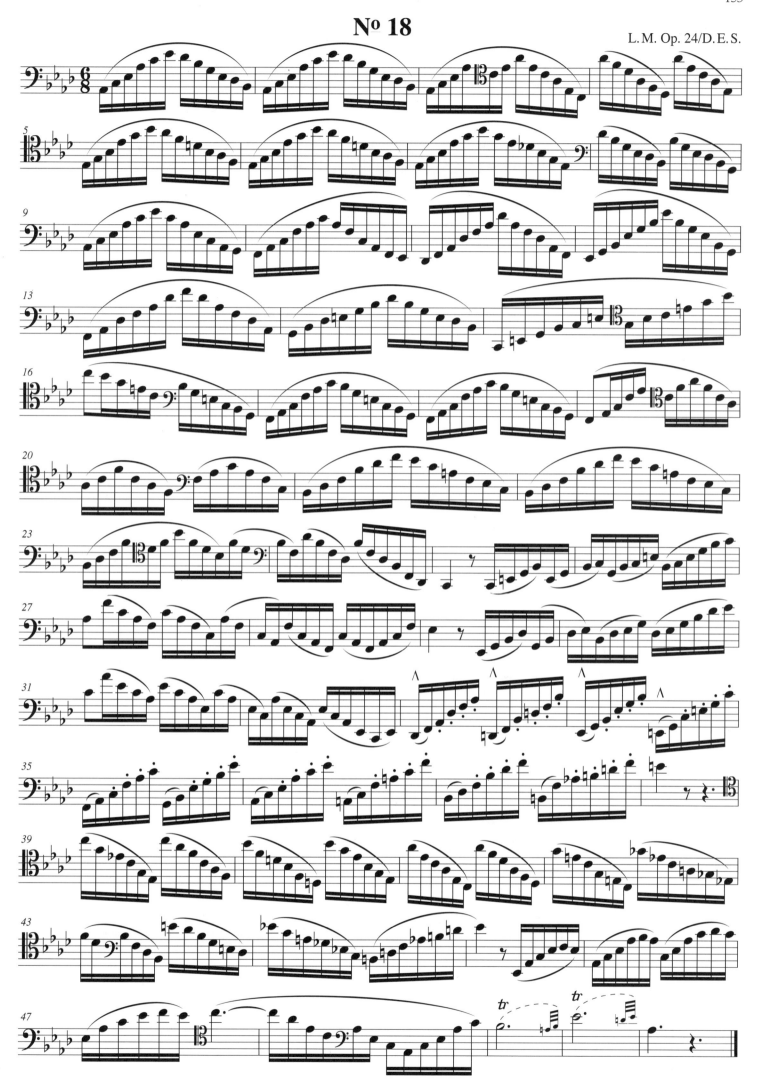

№ 19

L. M. Op. 24/D. E. S.

*The original edition had D♮ here, but D♯ appears to be correct.

№ 20

L. M. Op. 24/D. E. S.

Nº 21

L. M. Op. 24/D.E.S.

Nº 22

L. M. Op. 24/D.E.S.

№ 23

L. M. Op. 24/D.E.S.

№ 24

L. M. Op. 24/D. E. S.

№ 24A

Transposition of No. 3 (G major to G♭ major)

L. M. Op. 24/D.E.S.

№ 24B

Transposition of No. 4 (G major to G♭ major)

L. M. Op. 24/D. E. S.

№ 24C

Transposition of No. 1 (C major to C♯ major)

L. M. Op. 24/D. E. S.

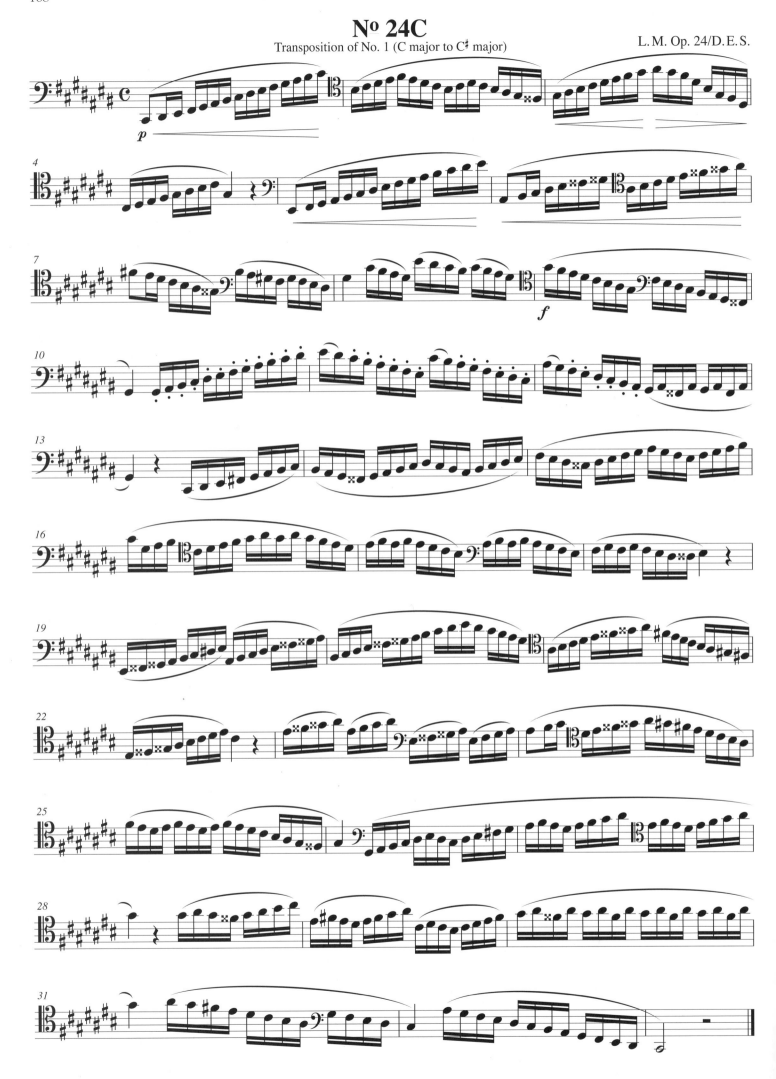

№ 24D

Transposition of No. 2 (C major to C# major)

L. M. Op. 24/D.E.S.

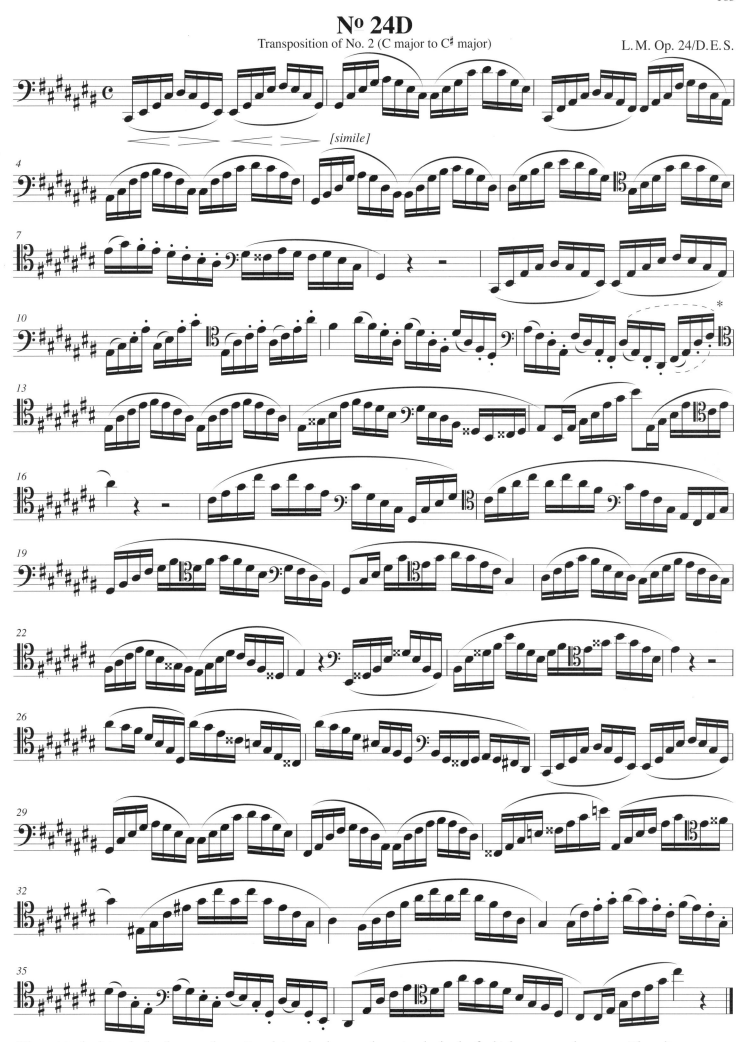

*The original edition had a slur over beats 3 and 4 *and* a slur over beat 4 only, both of which appear to be errors. The editor suggests slur two – tongue two as indicated. Some editions have C# for the penultimate note, but most have D#; the D# appears to be correct.

№ 24E

Transposition of No. 9 (B♭ major to C♭ major)

L. M. Op. 24/D.E.S.

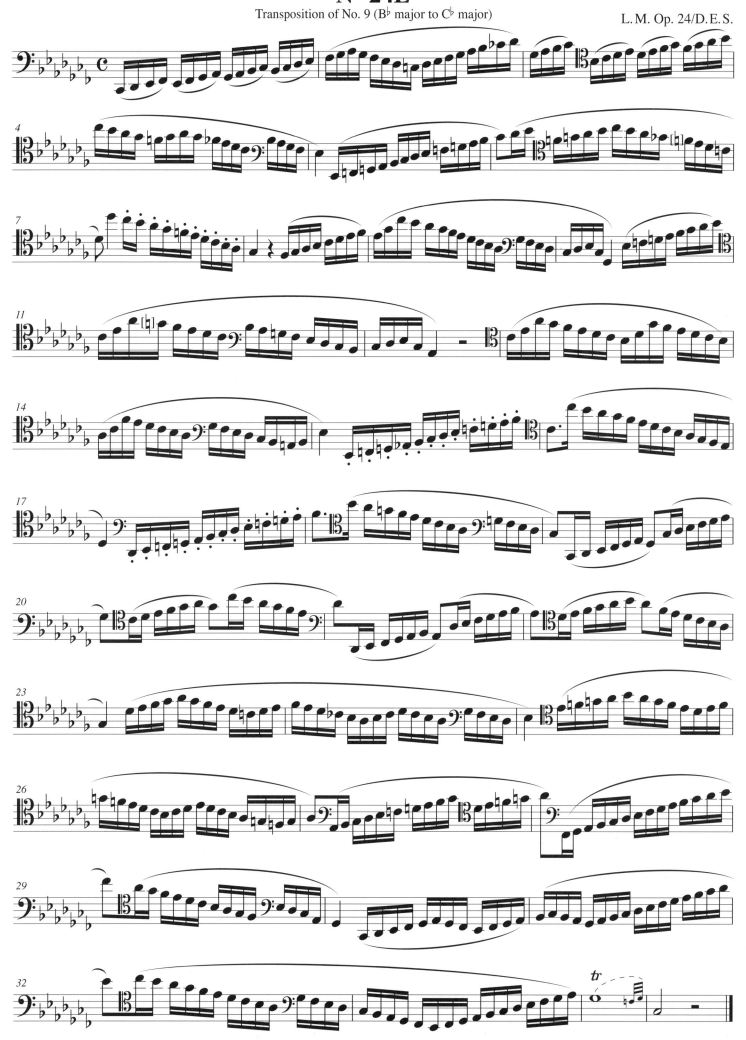

№ 24F

Transposition of No. 10 (B♭ major to C♭ major)

L. M. Op. 24/D. E. S.

№ 25

L. M. Op. 24/D. E. S.

*Kamins/Short edition has B♮'s in this measure. All other sources have B♭'s. B♮'s appear to be correct.

№ 25A

Transposition of No. 25 (to B♭ major)

L. M. Op. 24/D. E. S.

*Kamins/Short edition has A♮'s in this measure. All other sources have A♭'s. A♮'s appear to be correct.

№ 25B

Transposition of No. 25 (to B major)

L. M. Op. 24/D. E. S.

*Kamins/Short edition has A♯'s in this measure. All other sources have A♮'s. A♮'s appear to be correct.

№ 25C
Transposition of No. 25 (to D♭ major)

L. M. Op. 24/D. E. S.

*Kamins/Short edition has C♮'s in this measure. All other sources have C♭'s. C♮'s appear to be correct.

Fingering Chart

This chart includes fingerings for every note from B♭1 to E5. This list is by no means comprehensive. If necessary, consult the sources in the biliography for more options.

Tone holes that are blackened are to be covered; keys that are blackened are to be depressed. Gray tone holes and keys are optional. When more then one fingering is given, the first is the most commonly used or the one recommended by this author as a standard fingering. Other fingerings given may also be used as a standard fingering or for special uses as described.

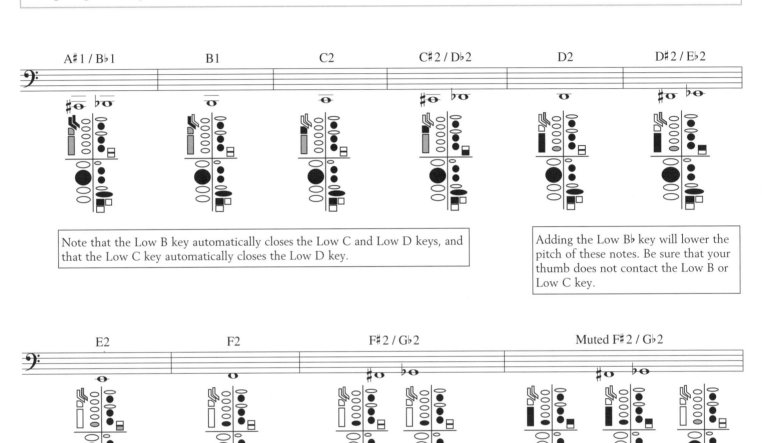

Note that the Low B key automatically closes the Low C and Low D keys, and that the Low C key automatically closes the Low D key.

Adding the Low B♭ key will lower the pitch of these notes. Be sure that your thumb does not contact the Low B or Low C key.

Adding the Low D♭ and/or Low B♭ key will lower the pitch of this typically sharp note.

Note that the thumb F♯ key automatically depresses the Low F key. Use the second fingering when F♯2 is preceded or followed directly by B♭, or to lower the pitch.

RH thumb depresses both keys.

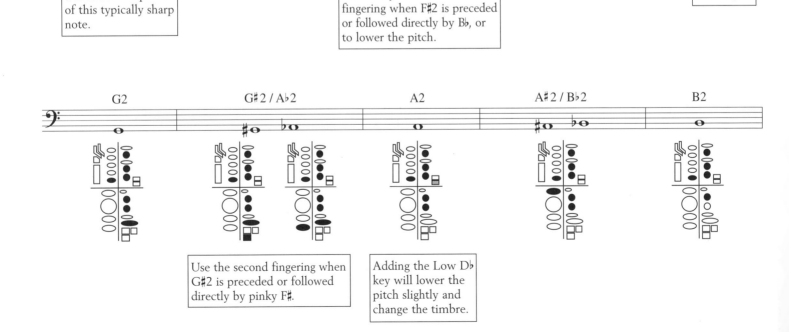

Use the second fingering when G♯2 is preceded or followed directly by pinky F♯.

Adding the Low D♭ key will lower the pitch slightly and change the timbre.

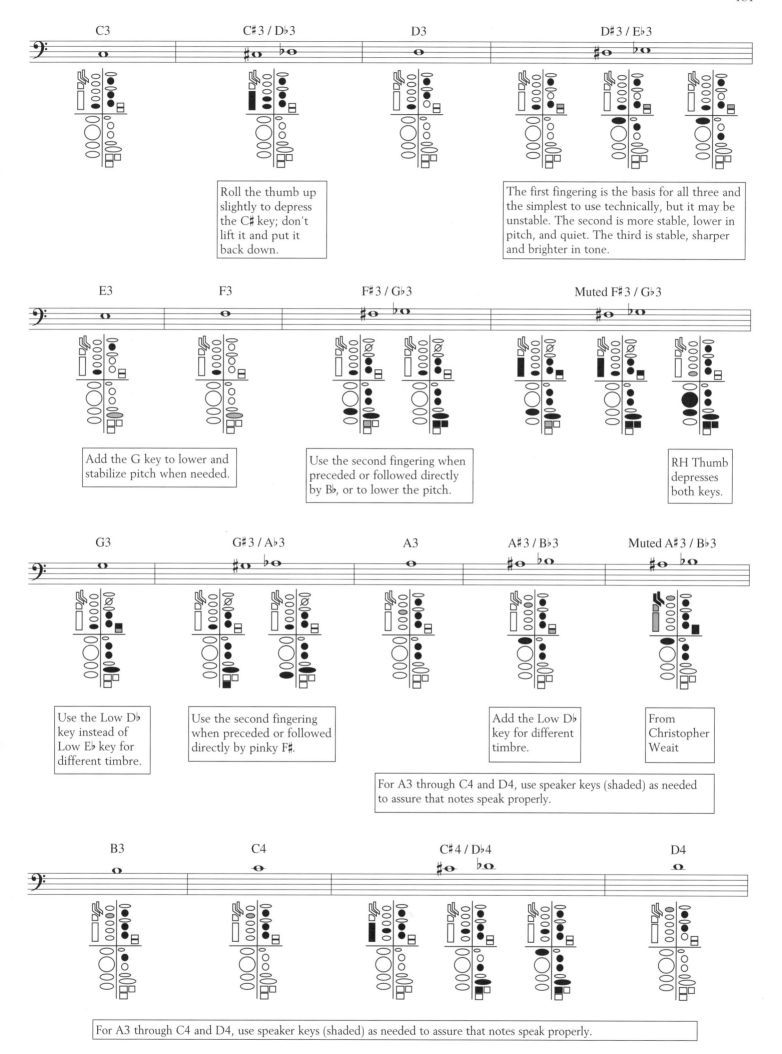

C3

C♯3 / D♭3

Roll the thumb up slightly to depress the C♯ key; don't lift it and put it back down.

D3

D♯3 / E♭3

The first fingering is the basis for all three and the simplest to use technically, but it may be unstable. The second is more stable, lower in pitch, and quiet. The third is stable, sharper and brighter in tone.

E3

F3

Add the G key to lower and stabilize pitch when needed.

F♯3 / G♭3

Use the second fingering when preceded or followed directly by B♭, or to lower the pitch.

Muted F♯3 / G♭3

RH Thumb depresses both keys.

G3

Use the Low D♭ key instead of Low E♭ key for different timbre.

G♯3 / A♭3

Use the second fingering when preceded or followed directly by pinky F♯.

A3

A♯3 / B♭3

Add the Low D♭ key for different timbre.

Muted A♯3 / B♭3

From Christopher Weait

For A3 through C4 and D4, use speaker keys (shaded) as needed to assure that notes speak properly.

B3

C4

C♯4 / D♭4

D4

For A3 through C4 and D4, use speaker keys (shaded) as needed to assure that notes speak properly.

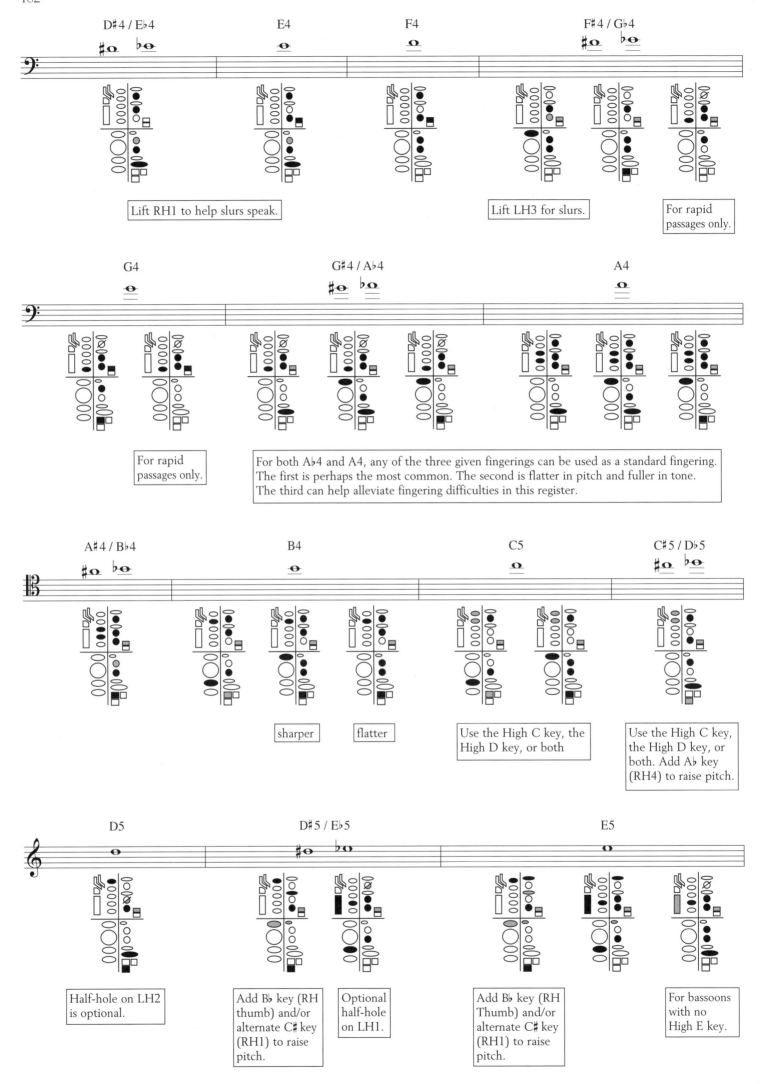

Trill Fingerings

This chart includes the fingerings to be used on trills for which it is not possible/practical to use the two standard fingerings. Some of these fingerings may also be used to alleviate technical difficulties in passages other than trills, but this should be done sparingly. When more than one set of fingerings is given for a trill, it is recommended that you try all the given fingerings to find which one works best for you in the given passage. It is almost always advisable that the first note of a trill be fingered with a standard fingering, switching to the trill fingering for the remaining notes in the trill.

This list is by no means comprehensive. It does provide common solutions to difficult trills within the range of this book (Bb1 to E5). If a trill is not listed here, it is either playable with standard fingerings or it is not possible/ practical to do on the bassoon. If necessary, consult the sources in the bibliography for more options. Bassoonists spend a lifetime finding new fingerings for trills and difficult passages. (Note: Most, if not all, of these fingerings are common knowledge among professional bassoonists. In cases where I learned of a fingering from a specific identifiable source, I've credited that source below the fingering.)

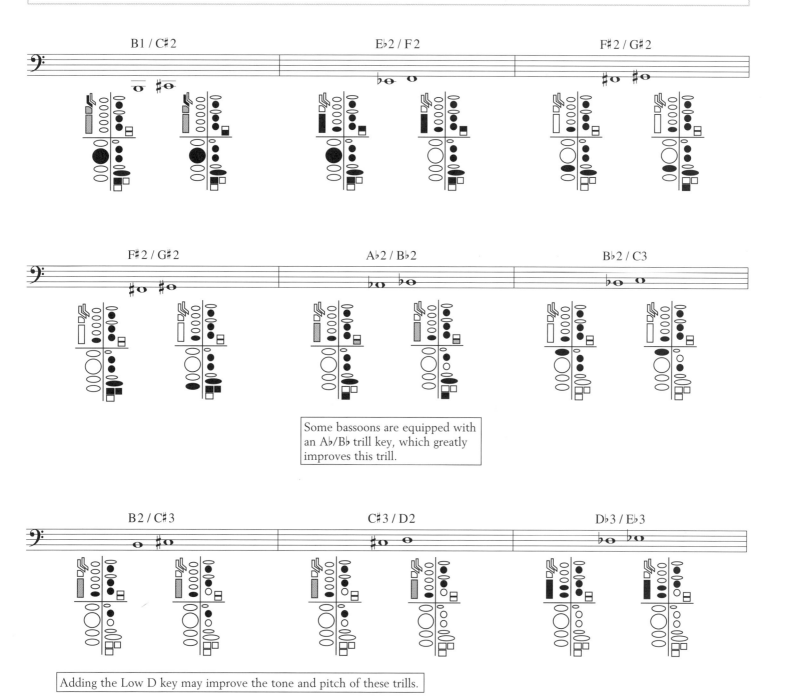

Some bassoons are equipped with an Ab/Bb trill key, which greatly improves this trill.

Adding the Low D key may improve the tone and pitch of these trills.

184

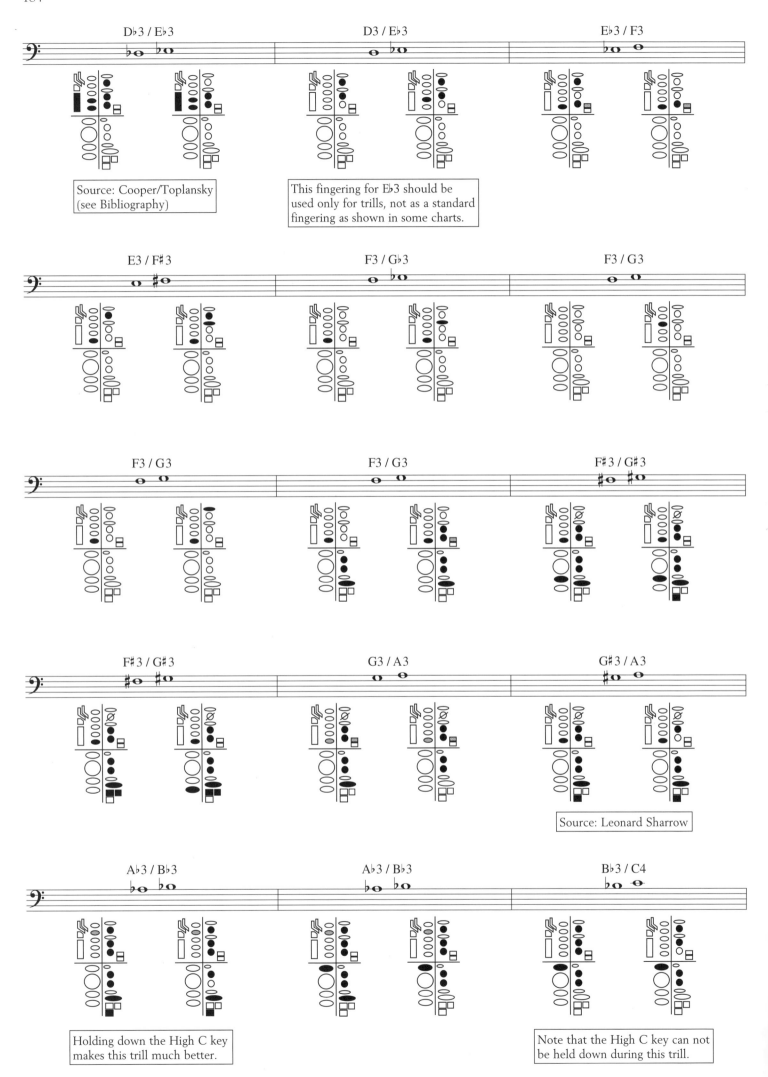

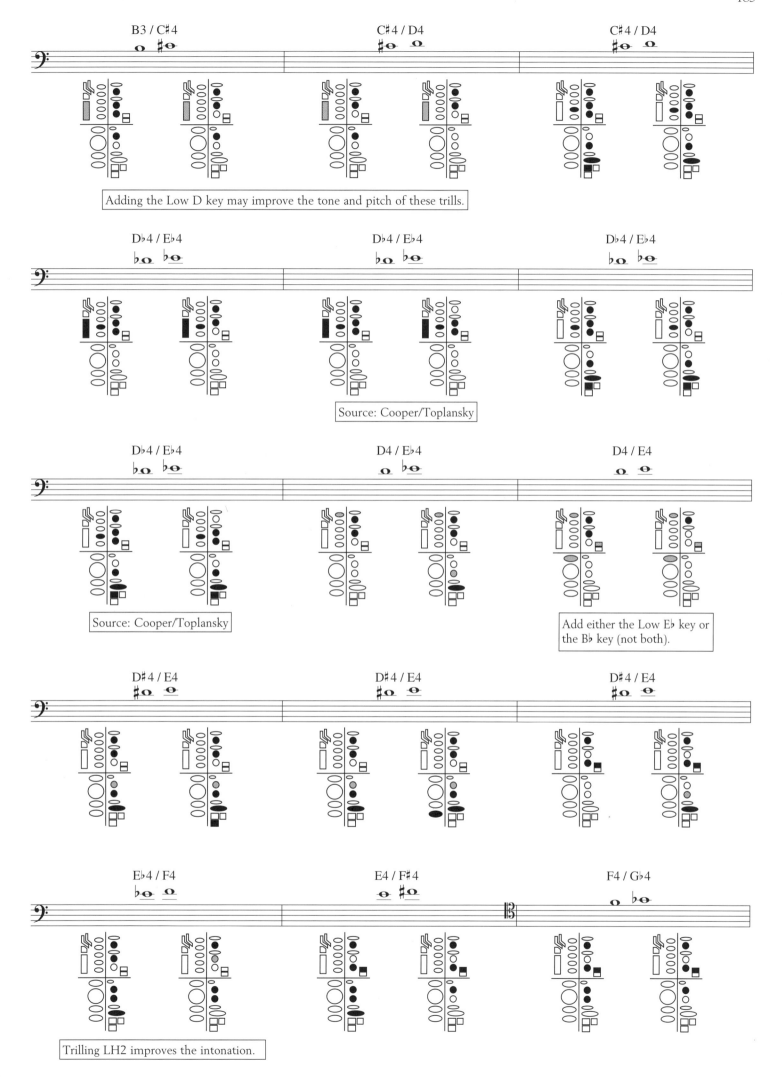

Adding the Low D key may improve the tone and pitch of these trills.

Source: Cooper/Toplansky

Source: Cooper/Toplansky

Add either the Low E♭ key or the B♭ key (not both).

Trilling LH2 improves the intonation.

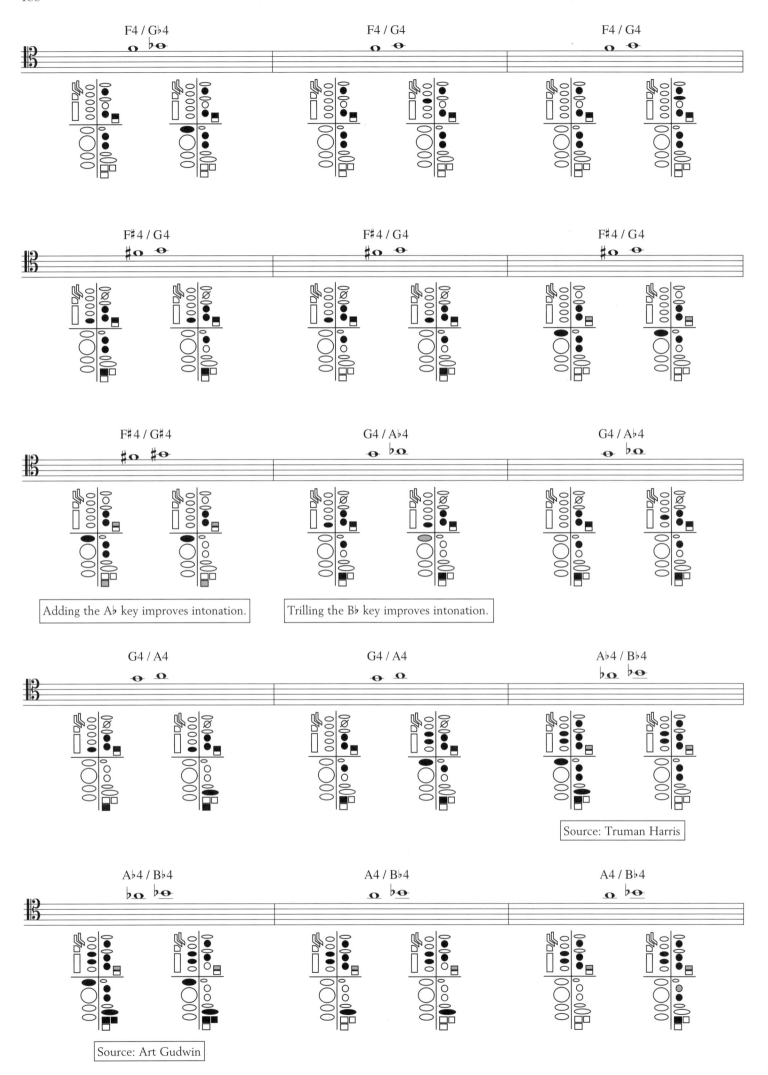

Adding the A♭ key improves intonation.

Trilling the B♭ key improves intonation.

Source: Truman Harris

Source: Art Gudwin

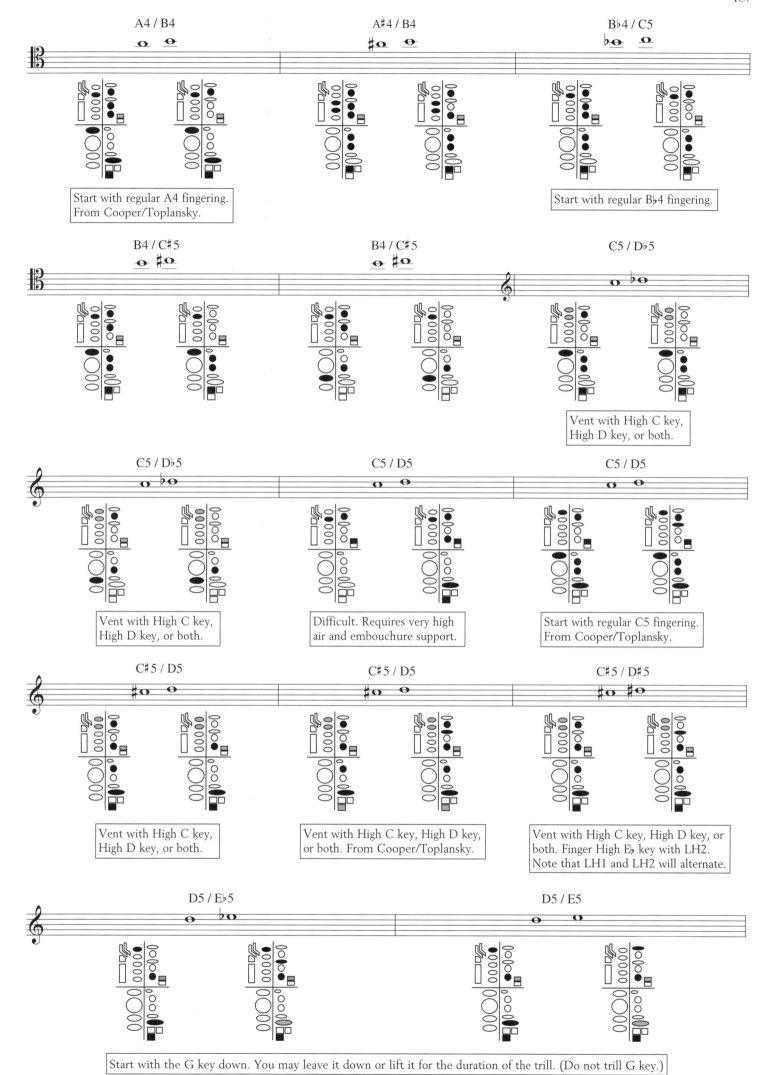

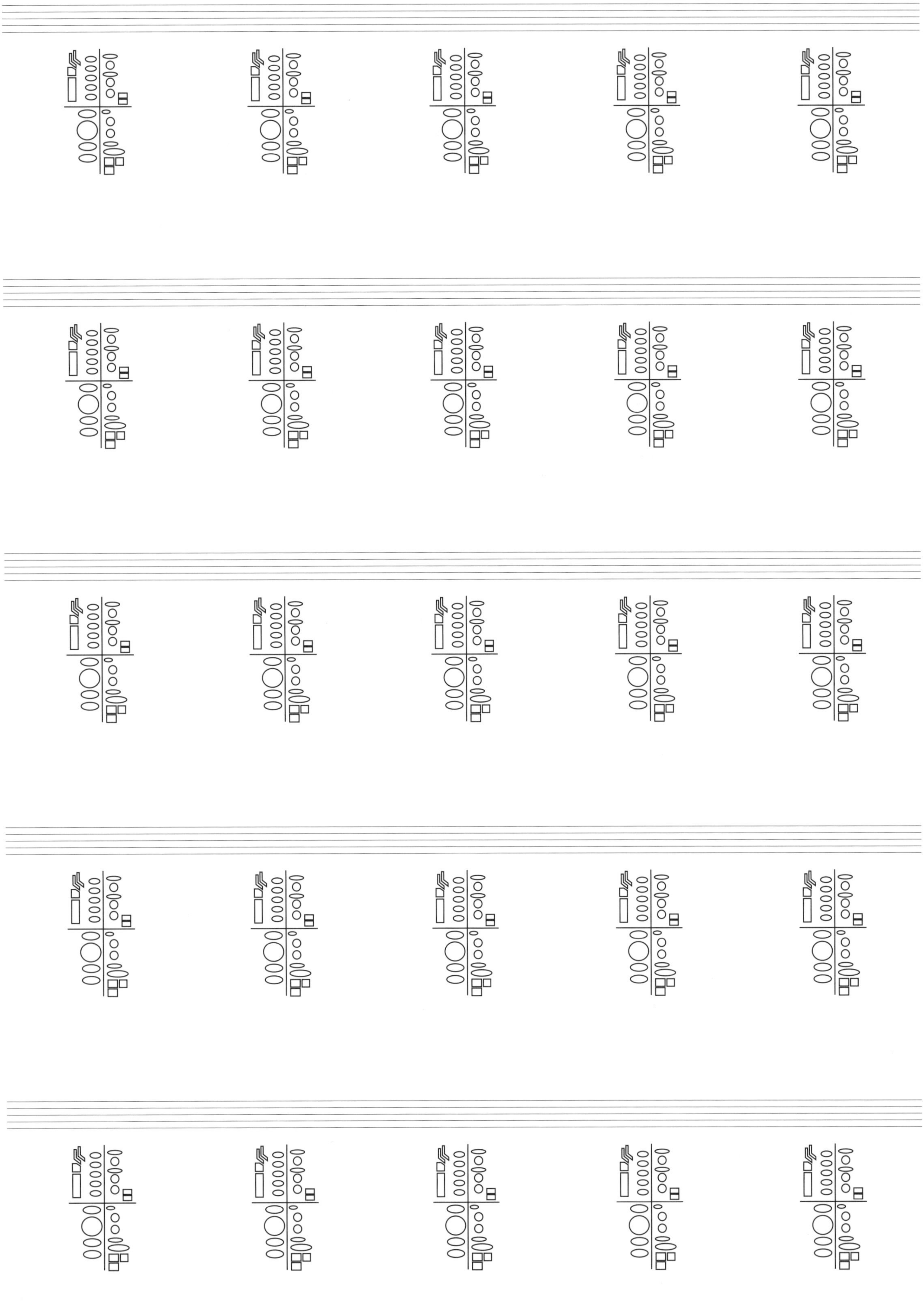

About the Author

Doug Spaniol is Professor of Music in the School of Music at Butler University's Jordan College of the Arts, where he teaches bassoon and courses in reed-making, pedagogy, theory, and chamber music. In the summers, he serves as instructor of bassoon at the world-renowned Interlochen Arts Camp. He was previously a member of the faculty at Valdosta State University and has twice served as visiting professor at The Ohio State University.

His bassoon students have enjoyed remarkable success, including being named a winner of the Yamaha Young Performing Artists Competition, and placing in the International Double Reed Society's Young Artists Competition and Meg Quigley Vivaldi Competition. Other competition successes have lead to concerto performances with the Indianapolis Symphony Orchestra, the Butler Symphony Orchestra, Interlochen's World Youth Symphony Orchestra, and the Kokomo Symphony Orchestra. In addition, his students have performed on National Public Radio's *From the Top*, been offered scholarships and graduate assistantships to many of the world's finest music schools, and have performed with the Indianapolis Symphony Orchestra, Louisville Orchestra, Indianapolis Chamber Orchestra, Sinfonia da Camera, and many other ensembles.

As a Fulbright Scholar, Dr. Spaniol spent the first half of 2012 in England teaching at the University of York and furthering his research and restoration of Weissenborn's pedagogical bassoon works. This resulted in a new edition of Weissenborn's *Advanced Studies*, Op. 8, No. 2 (which for the first time makes available all 60 of the studies as Weissenborn originally intended), and an upcoming edition of Weissenborn's complete works for bassoon and piano (including three that have never been published). In 1992, he was named a Marshall Scholar and subsequently studied with William Waterhouse at the Royal Northern College of Music in Manchester, England, where he was awarded the prestigious postgraduate diploma in performance.

Dr. Spaniol has presented masterclasses at the Royal Academy of Music (London), St. Petersburg (Russia) Conservatory, Indiana University, and for the Music for All/Bands of America National Festival, among many others. He frequently appears as a performer/presenter at music education conferences and the annual conferences of the International Double Reed Society. He also served for six years as Bassoon Chair for the IDRS's Fernand Gillet – Hugo Fox Competition.

As a performer, Dr. Spaniol has appeared as concerto soloist with Sinfonia da Camera, the St. Petersburg Classical Symphony Orchestra, Solisti St. Petersburg, the Central Ohio Symphony Orchestra, the Philharmonic Orchestra of Indianapolis, and Butler's Wind Ensemble and Chamber Orchestra. He can be heard as soloist on two CDs: *Bassoon with a View* (Innova 520) and *Frank Felice: Sidewalk Music* (Capstone CPS-8707). As a member of *Arbitrio* (with Alicia Cordoba Tait, oboe, and Bradley Haag, piano) he has performed throughout the Midwest, in St. Petersburg, Russia, and Buenos Aires, Argentina, and recorded a CD for Centaur Records (CRC 3013). As principal bassoonist of Sinfonia da Camera, Dr. Spaniol has toured England, been heard on NPR's *Performance Today*, and appears on CDs on Albany and Zephyr Records and the *Classical Music for Dummies* CD.

Dr. Spaniol earned a Doctor of Musical Arts degree from The Ohio State University and Master of Music and Bachelor of Music degrees from the University of Illinois. His bassoon teachers include Christopher Weait, William Waterhouse, and E. Sanford Berry. A Yamaha Artist/Clinician, Dr. Spaniol plays a Yamaha YFG-811 bassoon.